Around My House

Around My House

by

IAN NIALL

HEINEMANN : LONDON

William Heinemann Ltd
15 Queen St, Mayfair, London W1X 8BE
LONDON   MELBOURNE   TORONTO
JOHANNESBURG   AUCKLAND

First published 1973
© Ian Niall 1973

ISBN 434 51020 3

Printed in Great Britain by
Western Printing Services Ltd, Bristol

Contents

Illustrations

Author's Note

SINCE this is a somewhat introspective study of myself
and birds and animals I have kept and come to know
rather well—birds such as the falcon, the sparrowhawk,
the quail, the muscovy duck and the poor old battery
hen, and my days playing shepherd to a few mountain
sheep—I feel that I must explain in a foreword what
living has made of me. I have changed, and not entirely
in my old age. I was once a wild man in some respects.
I valued my own life but I am afraid I had little respect
for the life of other creatures. Now I see the only hope for
man lying in respect for all other forms of life, understanding that he doesn't own the world, or have some
priority in the business of living, but simply shares
existence with other living things. He dies and the worms
eat him. His death may be brought about by the living
things for which he had no regard, or by their death.
This is not an original view, I know. It doesn't matter

what philosophy takes my way of thinking and puts a name to it. I don't care whether I am branded a sentimentalist or not. I don't deny that I have been a barbarian. I am not repenting before I go to heaven. Heaven is here and life is integral, everlasting and, I think, in some form or other, quite indestructible.

I hope the reader will laugh with me and understand how deeply I became attached to a sparrowhawk simply as its servant in keeping it alive and nourished. I hope he will spare a thought for the hen that couldn't stand on her own legs, she had been so long in prison, and feel the emotion I experienced when the fox murdered my ducks, for I had little rage in me and I knew a fox can only be a fox. Bees are individual insects that pollinate flowers and even more so when they sting some tender part of the body. As a group they are like Goliath. They might make a brave man turn on his heel and run for his life. They are without emotion and incapable of love. They fawn on no one, any more than does the falcon. Their world is outside the fairyland of the average human mind, and they have what we might call a special dignity compared with man.

This book is my testament to a love of life and living things. I lived only superficially until I became involved with other creatures. I offer it to people who have never owned a dog, kept a singing bird, thought of feeding a duck or realised that life is not simply man's existence, but a much more complex and important force.

I

Myself When Young

LIKE all other small boys I was from the beginning imprinted with my environment and my mind was a sort of mirror of the world about me. I look back into the mirror now and in its Alice in Wonderland depths I see the things that shaped my present outlook. I see incongruous things and laugh at my innocence, but not without envy, for I doubt very much that the world has improved me. I remember relatives and friends with warmth and affection and I remember creatures like Wee Charlie, the pig. Wee Charlie was part of my infant world, part of the warmth and security of life as it was then. He was also the centre of a drama that left him fixed in my recollection of childhood, as permanent as a scar or a broken bone.

There must have been some ardent Jacobites among my father's family for they had a fondness for calling their sons James, Charles and Stuart. I had a great uncle whose name was Charles. I also had a Great Uncle Stuart. While I cannot think of a pet being called Wee Stuart the piglet carried the name Wee Charlie quite naturally. He was no ordinary piglet, of course. The others of his litter had no names. They were all Skinflint's pigs, part of the Irish Bacon Company's contract and destined to be shipped over to Ireland in due course. But not Wee

Charlie. The expression 'to contract out' hadn't been coined in those days but this was Wee Charlie's destiny from the moment he tossed his small head and looked up at the person putting skim milk into the trough. Here, they said, was a pig among pigs, a pig with impudence and that indefinable something people call character, finding no better word for it. I was taken to see Wee Charlie. We were both very young. At that stage in my life I accepted the fact that I shared the world with other animals and they were of different shapes and sizes. I was not as yet very articulate and my conversation was limited. I suppose I accepted a degree of lack of communication with all the creatures of my world, discovering daily some improvement. In time, without the pressure of 'civilising' influences a bond would have grown between Wee Charlie and myself. I am quite sure that man's progress towards self-destruction has been greatly accelerated by his disregard for the creatures he finds in the world when he first becomes aware of himself. But to return to Wee Charlie, he was short-bodied and short-snouted. His slightly transparent ears were large and had a peripheral 'hedge' or fringe of golden down, fine hair that could hardly have been called bristle. He was a clean pig, sleek and well-fed. I suppose he knew something about humans and read their thoughts. Why must man always assume that all animals are necessarily duller creatures than the least intelligent and most moronic human? I had not then the knowledge of the world that has since convinced me that this is laughably far from the truth for I have met more intelligent dogs, cleverer horses and more amiable, likeable animals than a lot of the human beings it has been my misfortune to encounter. Wee Charlie knew instinctively that he was noticed. He grunted and scampered round like a galloping buffalo. He raised his stubby snout and squealed to communicate. His small, bright eyes reflected vitality. He was happy in the pigsty and happier still to meet the animals who came to feed him and his brothers and sisters, to talk to him and stretch out a stick to scratch his small, round back. Day by day this relationship waxed and improved while the others of the litter, no less round, pink, sleek and well-fed, continued to snuggle down at their mother's side or lie in higgle-de-piggle-de fashion in the straw of their enclosure. Ears would cock and they would rise to their feet and squeal at the rattle of a can and they would all feed with the appetite of weaners, but only Wee Charlie showed that he wanted to be noticed and share a different world.

I say this on reflection, for I took things for granted at that time. My years were as yet too few for conclusions about anything, but every day we met, and day by day Wee Charlie grew bigger and more knowing, basking in admiration and demonstrations of affection. The agent of the Bacon Company had accepted the Skinflint litter. He hadn't seen it or counted it, but he knew the quality of the sow and the sort of pigs that would eventually be shipped to the factory. He knew that they would all be of the top grade, all clean and pink as pigs on a poster advertising pork sausages or the finest bacon. What he didn't know was the exact number of pigs for when a sow has a litter she brings into the world twelve or thirteen, give or take one or two, and finds some way of feeding the unfortunate one that has no teat at which to suckle its mother's milk. There was no question of Wee Charlie going to the bacon factory but where would he go in the end? The family preferred not to face up to this problem. It was like deciding how to get the harvest in should it rain from August until October. Time enough to face up to the problem when it had to be faced.

'Come and meet Wee Charlie,' my aunts would say, and the amused visitor would be hauled off to view that pig among pigs, the one with the knowing eye, the intelligence of a lively sheep-dog, a pig who wanted to be a friend of human beings, never knowing that man's role is to exploit the other animals in his world, that man is carnivorous and a predator.

The Bacon Company's contract contained a special clause, a date marked in for the delivery of the litter, fed and fattened to a set standard which, if improved upon might allow of the payment of a small bonus, but hardly made further fattening worth while. The 'float' arrived in due course. The piggery doors were manipulated to allow the orderly passing out of the now well-grown litter and their ascent to the vehicle by means of a ramp. This was achieved with a bedlam of squealing and much slithering and colliding. The men in charge of the float rattled bars with sticks, poked the tardy ones, beat back those who tried to escape. Finally they heaved up the barrier and took away the ramp so that they could begin the long journey across the county to the boat waiting to carry the pigs on a sea voyage to Larne.

'What will you do with that one?' they asked, looking in at Wee Charlie who had been railed off before the loading.

Wee Charlie raised his head and looked at the ring of faces. This had been a very different day from yesterday. The world had gone mad. The straw in the pen had been churned up and kicked into corners. Pigeons had gone clattering out of the loft on the gable. Cockerels had clucked their indignation at such disturbance. Now some-one wanted to know about him. His name had been mentioned. He stood all alone in the deserted piggery and he was, after all, a gregarious creature, a pig first, and then a pig who had found some communication possible between himself and human beings. My small boy's eyes filled with tears for him. I was Wee Charlie in the not too well-lit piggery, standing there in the middle of the straw litter, all alone, my brothers and sisters departed. Skinflint my mother was off rooting in the grass of the old stackyard.

'Oh,' said one of my aunts, 'we'll keep him.'

One often wonders where the seed of agony germinated and how trauma began. For my aunts and myself it was at that moment. Wee Charlie should have gone. The departure of the squealing piglets, his brothers and sisters, should have been delayed and the ramp put back in place. Wee Charlie could have been lifted over the tailboard and set down in the crowd where, looking over the milling company of pigs, we could have pretended not to recognise him and not catch his bright little eye. It would have been quick and the thirty pieces of silver could have been taken then and not later when he had, in the end, to discover that Judas Iscariot is in every man.

I plead the innocence of my childhood. Wee Charlie would never have died had it been up to me. He was, however, only put under stay of sentence and in the meantime fed more skim milk, admired, visited twice as often and encouraged in the illusion that he belonged in the human family. It was well known that it takes some sense and intuition for the points of a pig to breed one and a fool can fatten it. In fact a fool is the right sort of person to be given the task of fattening a pig, providing he pays for the foodstuff. Wee Charlie did well. He had the distillery bran and skim milk. He had mash and he had the leftovers and many a boiling of small potatoes. On these things he thrived until the head of the household looked at him one day and thoughtfully rubbed his chin.

'I think that pig is as good as he can ever be if he is to be a home-killed pig and better than he needs to be to get a fair price for him in the market. The time has come to either send him to the market or send for the butcher,' said Grandfather.

His words hung in the air and were met with no response. The canary sang. A cat purred. No one so much as cleared his throat. The moment of truth had arrived and all appetite had gone.

I remember I was happily eating my food at the little round sidetable at which I was always given my dinner

and I cried for Wee Charlie. My sobs had no effect.
A cat was a pet. A dog, though it was a working animal,
might be petted. I could make a pet of a hen that was
bold enough to put its head through the kitchen door, and
feed bread to any of the working horses. The pigeons
were mine. I was promised a black and white rabbit
and a rabbit hutch but Wee Charlie came into another
category. The business of making a living was something
outside sentimental feelings. A pig had a pig's destiny
which was the destiny of the lamb, the bull calf, the
capon, the strutting turkey cock himself, to say nothing
of the geese.

The butcher was a Mr Gunning. Whenever there was
killing to be done or slaughter was contemplated the
words themselves were never used. We 'sent for Gunning'
and Gunning, like Mr Pierpoint, knew his role. He came
with his steels and his apron, his knives and his cleavers.
He smiled the red-faced, fat smile of a butcher. Sentimental attachments were something he never permitted
himself and could hardly understand in others. Sentimental butchers die young, starving to death. I don't
know who actually conveyed the message to Mr Gunning,
but word was sent. No one knew exactly when he would
arrive but arrive he would, one bright morning, or one
afternoon when he had nothing better to do. I remember
his coming. My aunts were busy at the baking board and
the girdle, making treacle scones or potato scones. It was
afternoon.

'I declare to my God,' said one of them, 'Gunning has
come!'

And Gunning was there, trundling up into the court
in his ramshackle van. Wee Charlie's hour had come.

'Could you not put it off until next week?' my aunts
asked when Gunning knocked on the door.

Mr Gunning looked disappointed. He had driven five
or six miles to do us a favour. He would provide us with
pork, with leg and shoulder, with liver and spare ribs,

material for sausages, potted head or brawn, crisp, mouth-watering crackling that cried out for piquant apple sauce.

'A cup of tea and a scone, Mr Gunning,' they said, tense and uncomfortable at the expression on Gunning's face, but Mr Gunning would have no tea with buttered scone until his task was done. He had only called to pay his respects and the pig was in the piggery? Two women in a daze nodded and turned away. Mr Gunning tramped off to robe himself. They watched him go to his van and put on his apron, buckle on his belt from which dangled his steel, pick up his knives and cleaver and head for the pighouse.

'Would you like to hear the gramophone?' they asked me.

The gramophone played. I remember the tune because the choice of records was small. The phonograph was not long out of date and a gramophone with doors was a novelty. We could have played 'Drops of Brandy,' 'If you were the only Girl in the World' or 'Keep Right on to the End of the Road.' I had heard them all so often that they were never to be forgotten. They were my musical education if I had any at such a tender age. It was the end of the road and Harry Lauder sang it to make us sorry for ourselves, but brave. My aunts looked out and saw Gunning going into the pighouse. They knew what he was about. The gramophone played and they sat with their pinafores lifted to dab at the tears that ran down their cheeks. Charlie, Wee Charlie, the knowing yet innocent, trusting pig, would squeal his last and his blood pump out into a white enamel bath. As the squeal sounded above the noise of Harry Lauder's singing, my aunts broke out into loud sobs. We cried together, for small though I was, I knew what death was. I had seen a cockerel's wings flapping when his neck was drawn and seen the skin peeled from a calf.

Mr Gunning came to the pump which was just outside the kitchen window to swill away the blood that stained his hands, his arms and his apron. He looked up but no one looked him in the face. Later he came back to the door and knocked. The younger of my two aunts wailed her grief and hurried off to the parlour to be alone with her misery. The other one, white-faced and strained, poured tea and laid a few buttered scones on a plate for Gunning, the murderer. Wee Charlie's still warm body hung in the piggery with a gimbal between the tendons of his legs. He would hang to cool and, when the water boiled, be scraped or shaved.

There was something to be learned in this though I am afraid I have never been able to apply the lesson. One should never become so deeply involved with an animal that to contemplate its death is a torment. I think about that happy pig and remember him as vividly as I remember people I loved, and it does little to banish sadness to say that he was like any other pig, so many pork chops or ribs, so much bacon sizzling in a pan and making a man's mouth water. It doesn't do to become involved with creatures destined for the slaughterhouse.

There was no question of the big, black and white rabbit ending up on the table. He was too fine a creature with his nose and mask butterfly-patterned. He kicked his heels and bounced and nibbled the dandelion leaves I thrust into his box by the hour until he was almost buried by them. I remember going to the fête at the 'big house' and the rabbit being purchased for me. I am not quite sure whether he was bought in anticipation of the death of Wee Charlie or simply to please me. I was a somewhat spoiled child, I suppose, who basked in the admiration of grandmother and aunts. Not only was I to have a rabbit but a two-floored hutch with a felt roof. There would be room for other rabbits and the buck would have a mate. So it went. The buck was housed in his grand mansion. A mate was provided although the marriage broke up and the miserable doe died. I lavished affection on the buck. I toddled out to give him dishes of oatmeal mixed with moist tea-leaves, carrots newly pulled from the kitchen garden. The hutch stood at the corner of the shippon, in a sheltered situation, but despite this, after one bitter night of winter when the ground became iron hard, the buck died. He was almost certainly frozen to death. The world seemed very grim that day. The northern sky was leaden and the sun didn't show. I remember hearing the geese going over. They must have been moving south before the extreme cold that turned the water in the potholes of the road to something like solid glass. The frozen rabbit couldn't be decently laid out for burial. He was fixed in the hunched-up position in which he had slept his last sleep. I cried for him and everyone understood. He was not just a rabbit. After all, there were rabbits by the thousand on the hedgesides, the fringe of the wood and the open peat moss and they died. They were coupled and piled up by the rabbit-catcher before he shipped them off to Gunning who also dealt in them and paid sixpence for snared rabbits.

I mourned the rabbit for a long time and couldn't pass the empty hutch without being sad. In the early days of summer a solution was found. Someone digging out a rabbit found a nest of hedgehogs and took two of them, hardly bigger than cricket balls, to make pets for me. Once again I was to become deeply involved. The two hedgehogs, called Hubert and Herbert, lived inside the deep iron fender of the burnished range. They took over from the hearth cats and their kittens who loved the warmth and would sit there by the hour, snoozing and snoring or occasionally purring with sensuous delight. The cats could do very little to prevent the intruders from establishing themselves but snarl and spit and lash out with their claws. The young hedgehogs were armoured and soon discovered that they could take whatever blows the angry cats delivered. They also discovered the saucers from which these pampered house cats lapped milk, or even cream, and they drank their fill. At night, when the fire began to die and the oil-lamp was turned down the ashcan of the range was drawn out so that, much later on, in the early hours when the cold wind whistled through the keyhole, the young hedgehogs could slip into the ashhole and enjoy the warmth. Betimes the hedgehogs would clamber over the fender and explore the kitchen, trundling across to the dresser, sniffing beneath the armchair, taking more porridge than was their share when they discovered the platters put down for the displaced cats. Anyone who came down in the night would hear the hedgehogs scraping and scuttling about on the tiled floor. They were, alas, never to be as house trained as the cats. An early riser had to step carefully to put peat on the fire or blow flame into the embers using the bellows.

Hedgehogs that never feel the first chill of frost in the earth and have little need to store body fat against the harshness of winter neither make a nest nor show the slightest tendency to hibernate. Hubert and Herbert adapted themselves to a world of bustle and noise by day and the warm glow of the range whose fire never went out but they grew bigger and lost all timidity not only in the face of the biggest of the ragged-eared tomcats but of the sheepdog who would lie curled below a form, tired after his day's work. The dog knew he was master of the kitchen and he knew how to deal with hedgehogs but he never harmed my pets and all would have gone on in peace and harmony had a neighbouring farmer not come to visit Grandfather one late afternoon and stayed to sample his whisky. At their appointed hour for going the rounds of the porridge platters set out in different parts of the kitchen so that the cats which usually ringed them could all get their share, the hedgehogs awoke and scaled the barricade of the fender. The visiting sheepdog, nervous of our own dog, cocked his ears. His ruff came up and in a second he was there, knocking both Hubert and Herbert off their feet and snapping at their vitals as their underbellies were exposed. They died dramatically there on the floor while our own dog sprang at their murderer and began a fight that knocked over tables and chairs. Sticks were brandished. Ash floated in the air from the dislodged ashcan. Cats rushed madly into the oddest bolt holes and there was much shouting. I sat crying for I knew that the legs-in-the-air attitude of both hedgehogs and the blood, like crimson paint, that trickled down from their grey fur and through their armour to the black and red tiles on which they lay, meant that they were dead.

The old farmer whose dog had brought such disaster was not an unkind man. He looked at me, when his dog, suitably chastised and shrunk to half his former size, it seemed, was cringing under his chair. He delivered himself of a promise to see that I got another 'hurchen', which was the local word for hedgehog, two hurchens, in fact. They were on every road at night in summer. I must not cry. Everything had its time to die. I knew that only too well. Wee Charlie had had his time and the black and white rabbit his. Wee Charlie had died because his fate was to be butchered. He had been bred to that end. The rabbit had died because of the big freeze and other creatures had died then too, a waterhen on the field outside, a small bird fluffed up and drowsy, quite unaware of its surroundings as it stood on the frozen trough by the pump. What had happened to Hubert and Herbert was something different.

When this horror had diminished I was encouraged to give my attention to the pigeons. They were in a loft that had been constructed up behind a gable. The birds came and went through draining tiles set in the stonework. The loft had a trapdoor in the floor. It was possible to gain admission by using a ladder and I was carefully guided up to see the nesting places of 'my' birds. The pigeons were a fluctuating population of strays. None was particularly outstanding but collectively the birds were colourful, blue-black, red and white, red, pure white and almost navy blue. They lined the ridge and sailed round to drop down and feed with the hens. Sometimes new-comers would be noticed in the line-up on the ridge and I was always very excited at this. A new bird that was mealy or mottled pleased me enormously. I would rush away for the corn ladle and scatter maize to bring my flock down so that I could examine the latest recruit. The numbers would increase by ones and twos and then decrease again to my dismay. Occasionally a weak new-comer would fall foul of the regiment of cats that lurked in the shelter of an upturned cart or the doorway of a shed, and feathers and blood would mark its passing. Many more of these feral pigeons, for they were not in any proper sense homers, fell to the guns of neighbours who couldn't bear to see corn being gleaned by useless birds. My father had kept pigeons in his boyhood. He came home and whitewashed the loft, cleaned up the nest boxes, trapped and examined my birds and pronounced them poor stock, diseased, deformed, shot-scarred and not worth the name of homing pigeon. He told me that the kindest thing to do would be to get rid of them. I knew what he meant. Their necks would be wrung. The next step in the business would be to buy at least one pair of good pigeons and breed from them to establish homers in the loft when the young were fledged. All casual birds would be caught up and destroyed so that they would have no chance to breed and reduce the homing instinct of the well-bred birds. I couldn't bear the thought of all my red and white and blue-grey pigeons being destroyed, but one day, when I was taken on an outing, I returned to find that there wasn't a pigeon on any of the ridges, nor were my birds feeding in the happy company of the hens and ducks as they usually did. There wasn't a feather nor a drop of blood to be seen anywhere. The deed had been done. Up in the loft, two imprisoned pigeons, much fatter and finer in plumage than the birds that had lived there before, turned a bright eye in my direction. The cock bird cooed. The hen moved nervously on the perch. In a month, when they settled down, the hen was incubating two eggs. The cock took his turn when she came off the nest but neither of them could fly out. The draining tile exits were closed and food and water provided for the prisoners on the floor of the loft. In due time the fledged youngsters went out and in as the feral birds had done but now we had homing birds. They belonged in the loft. They might go missing but unless they were weak or injured they would come back to the place in which they had been bred.

Time passed and I went off to live in my father's house on the outskirts of Glasgow. I came back as often as mother and father could arrange it. I saw my pigeons had established themselves and their numbers had increased. Strays came and went but now the strays were easy to spot, not because of colour but size too, for the good stock my father had established prevailed. The bigger, fatter and more handsome birds were mine. The seedy, tattered and often dejected ones were strays and now that the homing stock was in residence strays would be chivvied and ejected from the loft.

I was a little older now. I knew that I couldn't own or possess anything that was able to fly free. In fact, birds or animals are never really owned, only kept prisoner by those who claim that they own them. I was shortly to know this, for we moved away from the Clyde and my native country, travelling south to live in a London suburb. Here, in the flat land of Middlesex, I saw a very different horizon. Few boys I knew kept pets of any kind except perhaps a dog, although a neighbour had a loft of pigeons. It was the daily flight of these birds that made me hanker for my own pigeons. If I could have them they too would turn and sweep over the houses, swirl in the air and clatter away again and my heart would sail free with them when they hung on the wind and came back in again on outstretched wings. My father understood. Soon he was making arrangements for some of the birds from the farm loft to travel south and constructing a makeshift loft for them. I was excited by the arrival of these birds. They were very special for they knew the lichened ridges of home. They knew the stackyards and the thistle-grown paddocks, the squalid ragwort that grew in the corners of the farm court, and the crowing of the cocks my aunts begrudged their ration of corn, but tolerated.

After the pigeons had been kept in confinement for two or three months my father decided that they would return to the temporary loft. They would never take off for the far north and fly the three hundred miles or so to the place in which they had been hatched. He released them one morning. I stood watching them swing round in the manner of birds getting their bearings. My heart was in my mouth in case they would fly away. They did. In a moment or two they were out of sight in the morning sky, they had diminished to dots that finally faded away. They never came back. I never had any other sort of pet to take their place. I was relieved when, a week or so later, a letter came to say that the pigeons were back on the ridge of the loft in which they belonged. They were, after all, true homers and my father should have known better. It was a long, long time before I was able to indulge a longing to have birds and other creatures share my world. I never kept anything as a pet.

2

My First Affair

MOST people are compelled to work in order to win time to do the thing they most want to do, I think. Only a few very determined people relentlessly pursue the object of their desire to the exclusion of all else, perhaps to paint a picture, live on a remote island or climb a mountain. I was not one of these, but I had promised myself that one day I would keep a hawk, breed golden pheasants, have fantails and a dovecote and awaken to the crowing of the cockerel. My involvement with falconry, to use the grander name for hawking, began when I attended a meeting of hawk-owners. They were a society concerned with all kinds of birds of prey. A falconer tends to talk of 'my hawk'. Indeed he may have both hawk and falcon and hunt both. The hawker is a humbler fellow, of course, but he loves his chosen bird and cares for her like a mistress. I stepped into a different world from the one I had known. I would have to have a hawk shed, a weathering ground, ring perches, blocks, leashes, jesses, swivels, even a hood for the falcon—a glove for my left hand, made of reinforced buckskin, so that the claws of my hawk wouldn't puncture the ball of my thumb and make the blood spout.

'What bird do you fly?' someone asked me.

I said I had no bird as yet. I was hoping to get one.

I must begin in the right way, they told me. A hawk should have a proper shed and not be kept cooped up in a backyard. It must be put out to weather on its perch or block in a place where it can see the world about it, follow the flight of starlings across the sky and keep an eye on the pigeon in the tree. Without this interest a predatory bird would wilt and go into a sad decline. Had I not seen the dejected creatures that pass for eagles in zoos, the meat-bloated, lethargic falcons sitting on old dead trees sprouting out of concrete and looking more like vultures than the hunting creatures they are really meant to be? I didn't need a lecture about the way of the falcon on the rock for I had admired the falcon, wild and free, on innumerable occasions. I had scaled a crag to get to its nest and discover that the last twenty feet are the worst, for the falcon has a wonderful eye for a nesting site and almost always finds an overhang to defeat anyone with less rock-climbing ability than a Joe Brown. I knew the peregrine's scimitar shape and the breath-taking stoop he can make as he comes down to strike a pigeon.

Falconry, said some of my friends, is one of the oldest ways of hunting. It is more commendable than sitting in ambush for flighting duck or walking the marsh pheasant out of cover to shoot him over the spaniel that followed his trail. Others sniffed and said it was all uncivilised. There was cruelty in it but there is cruelty in living and staying alive and our most refined way of living is barely veneered by civilised behaviour. We cannot escape the fact that life is a bloody business, though some of us insist upon our steaks well done! If we aren't hunting one thing we are hunting another. There is a basic honesty and no hypocrisy in the way a falcon flies at a grouse. The falcon can't win every time but if he kills today, and gorges his prey, tomorrow his half-digested crop will slow him down and he will probably fail. He can't attain the keen edge that results in a successful chase until he is in condition again. Gorged like a gourmet, he perches, fluffed up and content, drowsy and no longer interested in the birds that cross the sky. But day passes and the small feathers of his head and neck sit tighter to his bones. His beak becomes accentuated and looks more like the sabre in the hand of a galloping cossack. Now his pupil contracts and enlarges every few seconds as he focuses on objects far and near. He looks left and right and gently bobs as he takes range on prey he is about to hunt. When he launches himself his long narrow wings carry him aloft with the grace and speed of the running hare. He becomes as lethal as a bullet the moment he reaches the peak of his climb. Below him the rocks and cwms have all become small. Thousands of years have brought this hunting creature to this moment. The grouse on the heather bank cower and sometimes rise in a frenzied, whirring flight that ends in sudden death for one of them.

I thought about this a great deal. I had been thinking about it for years. In summer I would fish in the remote lakes of North Wales, where I now lived in what had been my parents' house. Once, in late September, coming away from one of these lakes, I put up five or six red grouse that fanned out from under my feet and rushed off with a great flurry of wings and cackling. At that moment I mentally put up a gun and shot one of them. To my astonishment a grouse fell. Its feathers drifted in the air and I must have stared open-mouthed for several seconds before the explanation dawned upon me. Far up in the sunset sky a peregrine had been watching the grouse and preparing to stoop. The birds had crouched on the heather bank, apprehensive of the falcon's descent. I had come up over the bank and put them to flight. The peregrine's telescopic field of view had excluded me. He had come down to kill, striking the leading bird, although in the last stages of his powerdive he must have seen me. A falcon strikes and turns up again in a way that must surely intrigue a designer of aeroplanes. When there is no danger he will drop with the kill and then carry it to a place where he can comfortably feather it. In this instance the diving falcon abandoned his kill and was away, two or three hundred feet out from the high hill in a matter of seconds. I picked up the grouse and took it home. A marksman couldn't have killed it more efficiently. There was only a small gash on its back.

That peregrine's kill had a great bearing upon my decision to get myself a bird, although I didn't know anything about the management of a captive hawk. I was intrigued to know how a hawk could be so confidently released to fly at its prey and recovered again afterwards. I knew nothing about 'manning' a hawk. In fact, apart from being able to identify such predators as the sparrowhawk, kestrel, peregrine, hobby, merlin and buzzard, I had very little knowledge of them. A buzzard sails, a falcon stoops, a hawk hunts the hedges and thick bushes. The buzzard's wings are rounded, the falcon's long and narrow. The sparrowhawk, which is a scaled-down goshawk, is short-winged. A falcon must have height in order to strike its prey. It tends to hunt open country. The sparrowhawk is a short-distance sprinter, relying upon a burst of speed, rather like the pike's dash out of the reeds to take fish from a shoal. The hawk hunts the bushes and thicker trees and cannot sustain a long chase, especially if its quarry can climb. The falcon's longer wings and consequent lack of manœuvreability make pursuit through trees next to impossible. What sort of hawk should I get myself?

My advisers dampened my enthusiasm almost at once. I had trained a gun dog once. Training a dog was child's play to manning a hawk. Looking after a hawk put a strain on a man's sanity, they said. The mistakes that could be made were legion. I might lose my bird from over-feeding, under-feeding or feeding poisoned food. I would almost certainly lose one with jesses on its legs or a trailing leash, which would hang the bird entangled in the top of a high tree. I might lose my hawk when its jesses twisted and it fell off the perch and then couldn't right itself. In the beginning I must see how a hawk was managed, perched, hunted and fed. Then I must begin with some hardy species which I could train to my fist without caring too much about my image as a falconer. But they talked about birds like the buzzard and the kestrel. The buzzard hunted voles. He also fed on carrion a good part of his time for the buzzard is like the crow and the vulture in this. He searches the hill and sails on the wind. He could never chase a grouse or a speeding partridge let alone a mallard. The buzzard can feed on young rabbits and hares, of course, for these have the habit of freezing and lying very still when the buzzard sails into view. Sailing aloft he slowly scans the grass and the bracken. His keen sight brings the hiding hare or rabbit out of its background and he drops upon it with his powerful claws and legs outstretched. The buzzard wasn't the bird for me, I said. I had a fancy for something that went through the air like a rocket. Something that killed in hot blood and provided the falconer with meat for his table. I fancied the goshawk for his incredible speed but I also had a feeling for the fast, waft-along of the eagle in pursuit of a hare going at full stretch. The eagle has the same easy flight as the goose. He travels a tremendous distance with powerful, slow-motion wing-movements.

I found friends who were pleased to have me come along with them when they flew their birds. We went hunting with goshawks on the Anglesey marshes. The gos is almost certainly the most highly-strung of all the hawks, wildest, most fierce and the most untameable. While a falcon's eye is brown the hawk's eye is yellow in contrast to the dark pupil. There is a certain advantage in this. It is hardly ever possible to anticipate the falcon's intention by looking at its eyes. The golden or yellow eye of the goshawk will betray its unease, its impatience and its determination to be off. The light in a goshawk's eye

is the light of insanity, some will say. It is certainly
baleful. There is no fear in the bird. Some say that the
main difference between the goshawk and the falcon is
the goshawk's lack of intelligence—the size of its brain.
Be that as it may, the gos when he is in yarak (an Eastern
term, I think, for the razor-edge of hunting condition)
is as wild as the tiger. When he is released or cast within
range he will overtake and kill nine times out of ten,
sometimes boring right through a dense bush in the
process, or rolling head over heels, talons fast to a hare
until the hare's life is extinct.

I remember my first outing and the way the three
hawkers asked my opinion on the condition of their birds.
I realised almost at once that jealousy is integral in
falconry. As with dog-owners, a man's hawk is always
superior to that of his nearest rival. The female goshawk
is larger than the male. A male gos, say the owners of
females, cannot really cope with a full-grown hare. The
female of the species is more dangerous than the male.
It takes a female to put down a mallard drake or a big
cock pheasant! The owners of male goshawks vehemently
contradict these assertions just as the owners of goshawks
scorn the way a redtailed hawk (a sort of American
buzzard) flaps after a hare. The redtail, incidentally,
when he does come up with the hare, kills it without the
ignominious flapping and rolling and tumbling that goes
on while a gos's talons crush the hare's spinal column.

The first flight I saw was at a rabbit. The rabbit,
disturbed from a tussock of grass, ran for the hedge a
hundred yards down the field. The goshawk was off the
fist almost instantaneously but there was a sort of anticlimax about it all. The goshawk so easily overtook the
bouncing rabbit and seemed to alight upon its back
rather than tumble it. The other two hawks struggled and
flapped and 'bated off' eager to be free and join the bird
sitting back on its tail and half covering the kill with its
wings, as though protecting it from some larger predator

hanging in the sky above. The rabbit was lifted. The gos, its claws firmly hooked in the animal's flesh, came with it. The reward was a small piece of meat. The dead rabbit, wrested from the hawk's clutch, was put in a bag. Off we went again, the understanding being that each hawk in turn would be flown at whatever was put up. The second flight was more exciting. A hen pheasant, flushed from a bramble bush by the dog (dogs are not good hunting aides for goshawks who are made frantic by almost anything), flew as fast as its wings would take it to reach a cluster of hawthorn bushes. The gos was away with a tinkling of bells that became more insistent when he crashed through the bushes. The pheasant, however, was down on the ground, running on in cover. The free-flying hawk sailed round and then went out across the field to perch on a pole. A goshawk flying slowly is a graceful bird but at a distance not unlike a cuckoo as he sits on top of a post. What now?

The hunting condition, one must explain, is something akin to hunger but not starvation. Starvation means weakness and serious loss of stamina. What is meant by 'yarak' is easier seen than described. It entails a brightness of eye, a particular hue of nail, colour of leg and sheen of plumage, and with all this, that restlessness that indicates the bird's eagerness to be up and away. This also means that a bird that is free can be lured or called back by its owner, providing he locates it quickly, otherwise the hunter may take off to get his dinner for himself. If enough time passes he may kill and, having eaten, no longer respond to the lure. He will sit perched and motionless. His bells won't tinkle and the business of locating and recovering him will become long and exhausting. A lure is a sort of mock bird, a pad of leather or cloth to which the wings of a dead bird have been sewn or tied, as well as some cords or thongs by which a piece of meat may sometimes be strapped to the lure. When the hawk is in sight, the lure, at the end of a long cord, is swung round in the air. When the hawk takes an interest the lure may be allowed to drop or be swung closer to the hawk. With any luck the hawk will pounce upon the dummy and begin either tearing it to pieces or eating the meat. While this is going on the bird's master will work his way along the cord and lift the lure to which his hawk is fast. Sometimes nothing more elaborate than the waving of a previously killed rabbit is needed to bring the free hawk back to the fist. Hawks have wonderful vision. The smallest piece of meat, held between the fingers of the gloved hand, can be seen from hundreds of yards away.

There were five or six flights that first day. The total bag was a rabbit. The third gos failed to overtake a covey of partridges but then the adult partridge is no slow-coach and a master of low-level contouring of the open field. I came home wondering about the stability of a bird like the gos with all its erratic flapping off the fist, twisting and turning and beating its master with its powerful wings. Such an unwilling partnership, it seemed to me, could hardly grow into anything worth fostering. A goshawk has only two aims, to kill and to be free. On the fist it was a prisoner, never to be trusted, and capable of taking a man's eye out in one swift slash of its beak. The relationship between the hawker and the hawk in this case seemed to be one of mutual fear or at best, love-hate. Was the goshawk never calm, never at rest?

My next hunting expedition was to the grass plain of an airfield where hares were abundant and something of a menace on the runways where they would squat, endangering the stability of a machine taking off or landing, should it run over them. We took no dogs with us but hunted a redtailed hawk and several goshawks. The redtail is a very handsome American buzzard. Its tail is magenta-coloured rather than red. Its plumage is handsome indeed but it is heavier than the goshawk by several pounds. Its feet are more robust and clumsy. When it takes off it proves to have a much lower acceleration than the goshawk but in fifty yards it will begin to gain ground. Let the hare jink and turn and the gos may over-run his prey. The red-tail adjusts his paddling rate and rows himself round to strike the escaping hare. His stiff legs knock it down. His broad wings beat once or twice and the hare is dead, mantled by the red-tail's wings. The red-tail relinquishes his prey with less anger than the goshawk and comes back to the fist like a hen perching. The frenzy and excitement of the goshawk's kill is missing, but the kill is quick.

I remember looking across the well-mown airfield and seeing a company of plovers far out on the grass, and hares, standing up with their ears pricked, silhouetted against the sun. The hares had no reason to fear the straggling company of falconers. They didn't know the restless goshawks bobbing on their masters' gloves, or the heavy red-tail sitting content as a parrot on his perch. The plovers rose and flew away. They knew hawks, it seemed, but then, they were migrant birds. The hares knew only the plain and the occasional disturbance of a skimming jet landing or taking off, creating a ripple on the short grass on either side of the concrete runway. It wasn't hard to get within a hundred yards of those hares but one or two loped a little farther on as we approached. The goshawks tensed and looked as fierce as the Roman eagle. The hackles on the neck of the red-tail rose and remained rough-looking.

'Ready then!' said the hawker whose turn it was to fly his bird.

His goshawk rushed away. The hares bolted in all directions and the gos, at first undecided as to which he could the more easily overtake, lost ground.

'Let the red-tail go now!' someone said.

The hares were moving out of range. The red-tail took off without apparent haste, beating across the ground, passing the grounded goshawk and going steadily for a running hare. The hare turned and dodged back. The red-tail dipped a wing, neatly cut a corner and they met almost head-on.

'Killed,' shouted the elated owner of the red-tail.

His bird stood on the dead hare, a little of the hare's fur in its hooked beak. The other hares, far off and slowing down, knew that they needed more than a burst of speed to save them from this buzzard.

I carried the gamebag. One eight-pound hare becomes a burden after an hour. We stalked on. The hares moved but we came up with them, one way or another, finding one in a depression in the grass and another hiding by the concrete runway. The goshawk that killed this one rolled on and on with the struggling hare. I was learning something about the goshawk. When its talons are driven in it is a reaction produced by excitement. The bird can only let go when it relaxes and it doesn't relax so long as there is movement in the animal in which it has fastened its claws. We killed several hares and then one of the goshawks struck down a crow that suddenly flapped up from a hollow where it had been dining on a dead rabbit. The crow knew that goshawk for what it was, although it had probably never encountered a gos before. An old falconer had told me that most birds have an inbuilt knowledge of hawks and falcons. A dove, bred in a dovecote without ever having seen a falcon, will fly to the cover of bushes if a falcon is put aloft. If a hawk is carried near to the same dove the dove will keep clear of bushes and immediately soar into the air, spiralling to climb as rapidly as it can. The partridge may not often be chased by the sparrowhawk but it recognises the goshawk, which is not a bird native to Britain, as a larger edition of the killer of finches and other small birds. It rushes away and flies very low the moment it sees the gos. We put up a covey of partridges that afternoon and the goshawk gained upon them as they fled, but then the bird the gos had marked dived into a gorse bush on the perimeter of the airfield. The chase came to nothing, nor would the partridge be flushed into the air to be pursued again. I watched it running like a moorhen, up over a stone wall and on across a rough field. The other members of the covey stayed on the ground too and try as we might, not one of them could be put to flight again.

There were many outings of this kind. I discovered that it wasn't impossible to carry a bird and fly it at prey and bring it home on the fist at the end of the day. A bird in yarak never seemed to tire of the chase but one that had been overfed soon became bored and would slow down and perch. I debated with myself whether I wanted to have a hawk or a falcon or a sort of half-hawk, like the American red-tail. Falcons are more manageable birds but they must be put aloft to 'wait on' while game is set and flushed so that they can stoop and kill. Very well trained falcons will follow their masters, flying slowly and steadily above him while he seeks game in the heather or the marsh, but such birds are not sold. Such skill in falconry is only acquired after years in the field but it is easier to fly a cook's hawk, as the gos was once called, and a goshawk can be used in hilly country, among thickets and leafy trees, providing it has been well-manned and belled. A goshawk, then, I told myself, once I had served my time and learned enough to be able to train a bird to my fist. This personal aspect of the business of hawking tends to be overlooked by the enthusiastic newcomer. It is possible to buy or take over a well-trained hawk and hunt it, but it is also possible to ruin a good bird and undo hours of careful training by mismanaging the take-over. In any case, no hawker worthy of the name cares to admit that he didn't train the bird he flies, living with it, sitting up with it, studying its reactions, making it his own like a newly-broken horse.

The 'furniture' of hawking consists of a variety of items from hoods to leashes, jesses, swivels. An expert buys only the swivels to which the jesses—the cleverly fashioned soft leather straps that are fitted to a falcon's legs—are looped and tightened. Jesses for a small hawk are finer, softer than those for a larger species and the smaller birds are given smaller swivels. The eagle is gaitered with jesses of leather strong enough to hold him and tough enough to withstand his beak should he determine to free himself. His leash is a long length of rawhide while the leash for a sparrowhawk is fine, soft skin. Should either the jesses or leash by which the hawk is tethered to perch become dry and hard the frantic efforts of the bird when it tries to take off may break the tie. A lost hawk produces a kind of dementia in its owner. He abandons whatever he has been doing and wanders abroad with binoculars, searching trees, crags, bushes and the open sky for a sign of his hawk. Perhaps he hears the bells or spots crows, or small birds acting in an excited way and knows then that his hawk is perched. With a trailing leash and wearing bells the hawk's chances of coming upon prey are so much reduced that it will often be weak from hunger and thus readily respond to its owner's call or the swinging lure, but the smaller hawks are harder to find. An hour or two of freedom may mean death unless the bird can rid itself of the trappings of the falconer and revert to the natural state in which it hunted before it was taken. Here again, there is a drawback if the hawk isn't native to the country. It may, by its size, colour and technique of hunting be conspicuous. Because of its familiarity with man it may lack an instinctive wariness that would keep it clear of the idle fellow with the gun who shoots anything out of the ordinary just to see what it is. The bells draw attention to the disorientated bird. They are very special bells of a pitch that can be heard a mile or so away. The experienced falconer equips his bird with bells of appropriate size fashioned, perhaps, by some Indian maker of falcon bells. Such bells cost as much as a pound a pair for the shaping of the bell and the soldering of its base can only be properly done by a craftsman. The belled hawk perches on the weathering ground and his master, out of sight, knows that his bird is there by the music of the bells. He hears them above the drone of traffic or the clatter of a harvester in an adjoining field. The same bells, however, may mean that the escaped hawk comes to a tragic end. A belled cat catches few mice. A belled hawk can hardly come up with feeding sparrows or a flock of starlings without the birds taking to the air well before he is within lethal range.

These were a few of the things I had to learn about and consider before I put on a glove and assumed the garb of a falconer. None of the falconers I came across was at all sentimental about hawks. Only one or two seemed to have a really close relationship with the bird they carried. I was inclined to think that there was a degree of cruelty about falconry even before I tied a bird on the block and left him sitting in the sun, captive like a chained dog.

'But you can't have a hawk and a pet!' I was told. I didn't like the word pet in any case. Making a pet of an animal or a bird that has no domestic lineage shames man and takes away the dignity of the bird.

I carried the hawks of my friends, learning never to be unwary or forgetful of the fact that a hawk wants to hunt and dash away, that it watches man carefully and continually. It waits to escape, even if it will willingly turn and alight on his fist once it has flown round him. This return to the fist, I was to discover, is the most exciting thing a novice can experience. The bird goes out and away, its long wings beating and its every movement in flight a kind of poetry and then it heads back, coming like an arrow for the gauntlet and the finger holding a small cube of meat. It never misjudges distance and only at the last minute will its tail splay and its wings act as airbrakes so that it can gently alight on the glove. The apprentice falconer comes to love the flight of the bird as much as anything else about it. He soars and sails with it. He watches it and sees the way its wingtips gently curve upwards and the primaries extend as it makes a graceful turn, hanging a moment or two at the peak of a circling flight from his hand and flying back to it again. The perched hawk looks him in the eye and there is no fear and hardly a trace of nervousness. Man and bird begin to co-operate with one another because the bird never takes food except on the fist. This is the secret of the whole business but the hawk doesn't fawn upon its master. The falconer accepts the fact that he isn't loved.

A red-tailed hawk, they suggested, when I protested that a kestrel could hardly take anything more exciting than a mouse, and lived mostly on insects, and a buzzard is a slow and slothful bird. I made enquiries about the American bird. A few were being imported, flown across the Atlantic. I might be able to get one for fifteen or twenty pounds I was told. I would have to tackle the bird as an eyas perhaps, put jesses on its legs, train it to the perch, feed it and finally fly it. One day, when I had trained such a bird to my hand and flown it, I might graduate to the goshawk, flying it at a mallard drake on one of the Anglesey marshes. I had a long, long way to go, they told me again and I might have quite a while to wait for my chosen hawk. Hawks tended to be exported from America in batches and not every exporter of hawks was reliable, and sent the bird after he had pocketed the money. I ordered a falconer's glove, bag and some swivels. I began to fashion jesses. I cleaned out the old summerhouse and put up a screen perch.

3

A Hawk on my Fist

IT was when I was all ready to go that a friend telephoned
to say that he had just received a very sick female sparrowhawk which, although I was no sort of falconer, I could
be trusted to nurse back to health. It would, in any case,
involve the daily discipline of looking after a hawk and
getting to know the bird. I knew the sparrowhawk of old
as a skimmer of the hawthorn hedge, a bird that came
and went, conscious of the terror it created, it seemed,
as a Tartar was conscious of the reaction of a peasant as
he rode past waving a sword. I really hadn't studied the
sparrowhawk at close quarters. I had seen pairs going to
and fro to a nest in the top of a thickly growing tree.
I regarded them with a degree of emotion that was
misplaced. I saw them as killers and common sense
deserted me when I should have known that they killed
and fed and rested and only man or a frenzied fox in a
henhouse killed for the sake of killing. I went to collect
the female sparrowhawk. She had a damaged wing. She
lay on her back and her needle claws contracted and
opened out as her feet jerked backwards and forwards.
A wild yellow eye was wide open and reflected terror and
after only a minute or two I knew how much wilder a
bird of prey is than any other sort of bird. The sparrowhawk is a delicate, almost fragile piece of bird architecture.

It weighs under a pound, an ounce over three-quarters of a pound perhaps, depending on the specimen and its condition. The male is much smaller, several ounces lighter and much more difficult to keep in condition. It must be weighed every day and studied carefully to see whether it is improving or declining, casting a pellet or sickening, for such a bird may die a sudden death in the hands of an unobservant but well-meaning 'bird-lover'.

How to keep a sick hawk when pulled down by damage to a wing and perhaps suffering from loss of appetite through shock? I decided first to keep my hawk in a darkened shed, to examine the wing and get it to perch comfortably on the screen perch I had made from a pole and a length of old carpet. A screen perch prevents the bird from 'bating' off the pole, coming down on its tethering leash and flapping up again on the other side of the pole, imparting twists to the leash and jesses and at the same time gradually tightening and shortening the leash as it is wrapped again and again round the pole. It is a simple and very old device. With a hawk that has never been trained to perch, the screen allows the dangling bird to scratch and scramble up again and regain its perch but there is one early danger and that is that the bird, worn out and fatigued, may lack the strength to flap up again and, dangling on the leash, will slowly die. A hawk left loose in a shed is equally vulnerable. It will dash itself against a window or rush madly to and fro when it is visited to be fed and perhaps inflict even worse injuries upon itself. I took the sick sparrowhawk away, my confidence diminishing with every mile we travelled. The hawk was wrapped in a cloth so that it couldn't flap or struggle and it lay in a small cardboard box. I really didn't want the journey to come to an end because I knew that before long I would have to come to terms with that wild-eyed bird and put jesses, swivel and the harness of falconry on its legs.

The business of perching that female sparrowhawk took much longer than it would have done had I had experience of such matters. It wasn't too difficult to get the soft calfskin jesses on its legs—the legs of the sparrow-hawk are not much thicker than matchsticks and a beautiful yellow. The claws of the feet are sharper than the sharpest needle and the bird doesn't release its hold. The 'hypodermics' go in all the way! The reaction to being touched is an involuntary one. Unless the bird's head is hooded in a glove which is pulled down over the greater part of its body, it will flap and become demented in its efforts to get free and putting even one little leather gaiter on its leg will be quite impossible. I knew this, of course. I was full of book-learning. All I lacked was practical experience. In one anxious hour I began to have the greatest respect for the practical. My sick hawk was at last harnessed and the leash properly fastened to the perch. The falconer's knot wasn't invented by Baden-Powell but by some man whose trade was hunting, away back in the days of Henry or Rufus. It enables a bird to be 'perched' and removed from the perch again with the minimum of disturbance. The knot doesn't slip but it releases the bird by a single pull on the leash and the hawk can immediately be transferred to the fist. My wild hawk only knew that it was a prisoner. It flapped off the perch and dangled. I gently put it back again. It repeated the wild bating off. I found myself a stool and prepared for a long stint of duty putting the hawk back on the perch. Anyone who had ever tackled the perching of a wild hawk would have taken me by the hand and led me away before both hawk and I went out of our minds. At last it came to me to leave things to nature. The hawk in the darkened shed would dangle for a while and then, when its jangled nerves steadied and the beating of its heart came to a slower tempo, it might right itself and not hang and die. I got up from the stool and quietly let myself out of the shed. I walked away and went down to the cottage and had my supper. I was involved with that hawk in a strange way. Perhaps I was bewitched, for I could think of nothing else. I could see its tail, barred fawn and brown, its handsome wings, its beautiful feather-trousered legs as it struggled and fought to be free but I could see it slowly spinning round, its eyelids closing as it died, hung by me!

It was very hard to sit it out. I said very little to the family. I watched the night sky darkening. I knew that there was much more to come even when I had my sick bird perched. I would have to get it to feed. I would ultimately have to let it sit outside on a ring perch, carry it and let it bate off my fist, let its wings, once the injury repaired itself, gain strength, not just strength to allow the bird to become airborne, but to make the high-speed dash necessary to catch its prey. The books said the last thing a novice should tackle was the keeping of a sparrow-hawk. Sparrowhawks were for experts. They were far too highly-strung, too fastidious to be managed by any novice. Just before it was time to go to bed I went up and looked into the hut through a chink in the door, using a small torch to see whether the hawk was hung or perched. She was perched! Her back was towards me. She turned her head. I saw the keen, hard expression of a startled hawk and switched off the torch immediately. She would surely sit on the perch until dawn? She had discovered how to get back before her damaged wing was too fatigued to allow her to scramble up the screen perch.

I didn't sleep too well. I was excited, apprehensive and concerned about the bird's survival now that I had her perched. This was no ordinary business of training a newly-taken eyas. It might be that the adult bird in mature plumage was past being gentled and hand-fed.

At first light I went up to the hut and again peered through the crack of the door. I could see the hawk sitting on the perch with the timelessness about it that is also to be seen in a perched owl. There is no clock in the world of creatures other than man, save the digestion of the stomach content or the crop. The sun rises, the cock crows and birds twitter. A hawk sits motionless until it knows its hunger and then, if it is a fit bird, it abruptly shoots itself from twig or branch and slides away across the open country on the well-defined circuit of its hunting territory. My tethered bird had no appetite. Shock and the strangeness of its surroundings had reduced its needs. The brain of a hawk is small. It is a much less intelligent bird than a falcon which probably accounts for its extreme wildness. It reacts like a highly bred and unbroken blood horse. I noted the dropped wing just before I opened the door and from that moment on the hawk was wild. I saw myself coming a thousand times and finding it no more ready to accept my presence. I took the leash from the pole of the screen perch and drew the bird to me. It beat my face with its wings and then, when it had little strength left it hung, upside down, its beak open as it panted. I felt the terror transmitted to my own nervous system. I understood the sensitivity of the wild hawk. I gently lifted it and put it back on the perch. It flapped off. I retreated, closing the door. My thumb was bleeding. One of the curved claws had gone deep into my flesh but I had felt nothing. I stood wondering whether the kindest thing I could do would be to kill that wretched hawk, put it out of its misery and have peace myself. Four or five times during the day I went quietly back to the hut and peered in. The hawk faced this way and then that way, having changed its position on the perch. I came with a mouse which I had trapped and entered the hut. It was a long time, perhaps half an hour, before the flapping stopped and the bird scrambled back up onto the perch. An age afterwards I slowly offered the mouse. The bird stood straighter on its legs. Its neck seemed to arch back. Its eyes widened. It flapped and dangled again. I took a small leather thong and tied the mouse on the perch as securely as I could and went away. The hawk remained dangling but I knew it could right itself and would, once I had gone away. Just at dusk I peered in again. The mouse was untouched. The hawk stood still on the perch, ignoring its food.

Anyone who wants first of all to be a falconer must master the qualms he may have about the inherent cruelty in starving a hawk and overcoming its terror by allowing it to starve. I have come to know this so well that I would say that falconers are parasitical upon the hawk and not everyone with all the know-how in the world is temperamentally suited to handling a bird of prey in the hunting field.

The following morning the hawk hadn't touched the mouse but she was staring at it. She would either eat it or become so weak that she would die, I thought. There and then, without flapping and as I stepped into the hut, she reached out with her beak and struck at the limp mouse. A talon took hold of the dead creature like a murderer's strangle-hold on the throat of his victim. The hawk fed, tearing the mouse to pieces. I retreated again because once the remains slipped out from the loop of leather thong the bird knew me again and flapped madly. A little later I peered through the crack of the door once more. Her crop stood out on her breast so that she reminded me of a tumbler pigeon. She had her eyes closed. Time and patience are the thing that matter most in handling any kind of wild creature. The hawk wouldn't feed the next day but the day after that she stared hungrily at the second mouse which I held in my hand. I didn't tie this one to the perch but put on a glove and took the hawk in my hand, holding the mouse in the other hand. The wildness was undiminished. She flapped and hung upside down but at length, after gyrating for what seemed an eternity, she perched on my fist even though she immediately flapped off again. After an hour she would come back up almost at once. She was still wild-eyed, still in terror of me, but hungry. At last with a sudden dart of her head she seized the mouse and held it in her beak. I was delighted, except when she let it fall to the floor and showed no interest in finding it or looking down. I gently lowered myself and picked up the mouse. This time she took it, pinning it with her claws. She looked left and right and then looked down. A minute or two passed and she began to feed! I was still a terror to her, but she wouldn't feed again except on my hand. The books said this, but I knew it now as I hadn't known it before. When she had done feeding she was wild again. I got her back onto the screen perch and slowly retreated to sit and watch her. While I kept perfectly still she ignored me completely. She looked through the window of the hut which adjoined her perch. She could see the birds that flew across the little orchard and the jackdaws that sailed out from the cliff. A hawk is a tireless watcher of the sky and what passes over, an eternal spectator when fed, a restless almost lunatic creature when tethered and hungry.

The following day I fed her again in the same way. In a week she would step from the perch onto my gloved hand and seize what I had brought for her even before she was settled. I found dead thrushes and other small birds scattered here and there along the road. I drove looking for road casualties that would feed the hawk. I trapped mice. I set up a cage to breed mice. I thought about how the hawk fed and what she needed to bring her into condition. I walked her outside on my fist and she bated off and went mad to leave me, but her drooped wing was no better and until it mended she wouldn't have the speed to catch her own bird or mouse. I put her on the ring perch, a falconer's device for perching hawks whose long tails would otherwise become worn and damaged if they were simply tethered to a pin on the grass. She had to be taught to perch and for days she would sit in the grass and flap wildly when I went to pick her up and put her on the ring. I loved to see her take the dead bird I offered, hold it in one claw and quickly and expertly feather it, the thing a hawk always does before beginning to eat. She would begin on the head of the bird once it was feathered, ripping away the skull bones and eating the brain. If a small feather adhered to her beak she was capable of flicking it off, no matter how sticky and adhesive it seemed to be. When she had eaten the breast of the bird she would remove and discard part of the intestines. The heart and liver were eaten, even the legs and wingtips were bolted down. She looked comic with a dead bird's claw protruding from her hooked beak. People who saw her were horrified, even disgusted. I didn't react in this way myself. Hawks were feeding like this at every hour of the day, wild or tame birds. Our relationship had improved. She would allow me to come within twelve feet without losing her nerve but she always flapped and bated off my hand both when I put her out or took her in. There was a slight improvement in the drooped wing. The colour of legs and sear was brilliant. She was casting pellets and I was careful to see that she was shaded from the sun and never left out in a shower, which amused some of my friends. I thought she needed some variety in her diet and one day gave her a small piece of the liver of a hare before going off to join some of my hawking friends who were hunting on the island across the estuary. When I came home late that night I hurried to perch my bird but to my dismay she lay in the grass on her back. Her feet were thrust up. She was quite dead. I knew misery. I had come to love that hawk.

Perhaps it should have ended there, but the whole business was in my blood. I would have a hawk flying to my hand. I would master the sparrowhawk, the most difficult of them all. I began to believe that despite everything anyone said about the untameability of the lesser hawks, I could tame one. I could bring it to me without starving it. I could establish a relationship with this small-brained, lunatic bird by getting to understand the level upon which it existed. Communication was impossible except in a most elementary fashion. I must cease to be a source of terror to the bird. I must be inwardly calm and suppress the slightest reaction of irritation because I was handling a most delicate instrument, a creature far more attuned to life and the moods of living things than I was, something with a disconcerting telepathic knowledge of me as a human being. In less than a week the same friend telephoned to say that he had been brought another sick bird, a sparrowhawk, but this time a male no bigger than a thrush. I must understand that the males were even harder to manage. They were so small and slight that their metabolism was of such delicate balance that they couldn't be brought through winter by a novice. Most falconers who handled such a bird set it free in good time to hunt for itself and gather the fat and vitamins it needed to survive in the cold, bleak days of January and February. The female sparrowhawk is more brown than grey on the back and her front, throat and breast are more distinctively marked, barred grey and white, while the male's back is slate grey and his less distinctively barred frontal feathering is rufous in colour. His wingspread is two inches less than that of the female. Falconers call the male by a special name. It is known as a musket. Being so small it is thought to be hardly worth training as a hunting bird. Fierce and fiery though it may be, its quarry is generally something not much larger than the common sparrow. I wasn't really interested in hunting a musket, even if I trained it to my hand and brought it through the winter which would be enough of a challenge even for an expert.

The musket seemed less hysterical than the female I had kept and let die of a surfeit of poisoned hare's liver, but he was docile because he was shocked and I had a suspicion that he had been brought low by having to live on things less commonly taken by hawks. I began the same process of perching and putting him out to weather.

He was even more fascinating than the female because of his diminutive appearance. I weighed him every day on a specially adapted weighing machine, as I had done the female. Weight is the barometer of hawk-health. A bird that refuses to eat is certainly sick but equally in danger is the over-fed bird, made sluggish by its keeper. It too may keel over, especially if fed things which lack the ingredients for pelleting which is essential to the species. My little musket fed with great ferocity once he came to my hand. I found him an endearing bird because of the coolness of our relationship and the way he would hop off the perch onto my hand to be fed and hop back again immediately he was ready to wipe his beak. Wiping the little sabre of a blue-grey beak is one of the habits of the sparrowhawk as soon as it has fed. It seems to love to keep its beak free from anything that might adhere to it. Perhaps the smallest thing interferes with the line of vision, or it may be that even while the hawk is capable of trailing out the intestines of a bird like hanks of piping it really is a fastidious creature. Day by day I became fonder of the musket. It was his smaller size and a sort of self-assurance that won me. I would enter the hut and he would bob to get the range of my gloved hand as I reached forward as far as I could and released him. With the uncanny accuracy of hawks he would be on my hand in a second. A glove wasn't necessary any more. All tension had gone. He was daily becoming stronger. I walked him out, a short distance at first, and then farther and farther until we were walking five miles, over drystone walls, through close-growing, thick hedges, uphill and down. I could jump a ditch and he remained firmly perched on my fist. I could bring him to my cheek and his eye looked into mine and with it all he was no more a pet than the wild, free-flying gyr falcon or the goshawk.

When we walked I would watch him as he inspected the bushes through which we passed. He'd look up and saw a flight of pigeons passing over or a wild duck in

flight and I knew by the tightening of his small talons
that he was reacting with the excitement of a born hunter.
Had he been big enough he would have killed an elephant.
He was a tiger in miniature. He looked through bushes.
He missed nothing. I began to see how blind I was and
how unobservant. The hawk's talons, tightening on my
hand, told me to look and I looked, but my mind was
slow and my eye dull and my head wouldn't turn to scan
the area through which some wild and fast bird was
flying. Winter had come and although he had come on
so well I knew that the scarcity of small migrant birds
and the territorial ways of predators would mitigate
against my small hawk's survival even if I could face the
wrench of parting with him and letting him go free.

There was snow that winter. Redwings took shelter
under holly bushes and among the bare stalks of old
blackberry clumps where, in the extreme cold, they died.
I gathered a few and kept them for the musket. I watched
him devour the skins of his 'victims'. What fat they had
kept him warm. Now I was like a hawk myself, going
about in search of food for him. I put down glass bottles
with tiny bits of cheese or chocolate in them, laying them
on their side but propped up so that a mouse venturing
down the slippery slope to get the chocolate couldn't
get up again and the hawk had what I called a hot meal.
Barbaric as this may sound, it is no more than happens
in the wild. I worked hard because I loved the bird and
because his survival was a challenge I couldn't refuse.
By the end of winter he was still there on his screen perch,
weighing his full fighting weight, and a fraction of an
ounce more on days when he didn't exercise. In the
spring I put him outside, perching him on a line or
creance of about a hundred yards long. I carefully laid
the line out so that if he took off in my direction he
wouldn't be brought down by a tangle slipping round
some small obstruction on the ground such as the stalk
of a weed. Seventy yards away I took the dead bird, a

pathetic little bluetit that had died in collision with our
electricity wires, and held it in my hand. A human being
could never have recognised it for what it was, but the
musket knew. I called. He came to me at top speed.
Head-on he looked like something in a slow-motion film
at the moment he reached my hand, but at once he was
busily engaged feathering the bluetit, occasionally pausing
for a second to look at the small feathers drifting away on
the breeze until he plucked the bird bare and devoured it.
I knew that in a matter of a week or so, if I fed him well
and gave him all the flying exercise I could, he would be
able to hunt and fly free.

I had him on my hand one afternoon when a blackbird
settled on the slope below the hut. His excitement at
this was always intense and on this occasion I drew the
leash out of the swivels and let him fly. He rushed at the
blackbird, swung in a half circle, knocked feathers from
his target and flew straight back to me because the
blackbird escaped into the thick stems of the wych-elm
hedge. I had done what no really responsible falconer
should do, allowed the bird to fly encumbered by jesses
and swivels which, had they caught in the high top of a
tree, would have caused him to hang there and die. Next
time he was allowed to fly free he would fly without jesses
or swivel!

I might not be a very experienced falconer. I had
worked entirely on my own with very little advice from
anyone else and too much book-learning for my mental
digestion, but I had brought the smallest hawk through
a severe winter and flown it free. The days ahead filled
me with a sense of gloom. Soon I would have to put
myself to the test and prove that I cared for the hawk
flying free more than I cherished any image of myself
as a robust fellow with a hawk on his fist. A man with such
a small hawk can hardly imagine himself robust and virile.
The hawk on my fist wasn't part of my mental image of
myself. It was something much more. It was a creature I

understood better than anything I had ever adopted or kept, even my faithful spaniel, Nick.

The freeing of the small hawk was put off from day to day. I suffered anguish. I thought, because I wanted to think so, that he would sit on a tree and mope and then starve to death. It was a wonderfully sentimental indulgence but I steeled myself at last and one bright morning I cut the jesses from his slender legs and let him slip away into the sunshine with no quarry in sight. He never looked back. He swam in the scented air of the morning with fast and powerful wingbeats. I hadn't imprinted him with an image of myself as anything else but a perch upon which there was food. Away he went. I was sorry for myself in that moment, but as the day passed I became happier, enjoying a warm feeling at the thought of the musket sitting on a branch feathering the first thing he had chosen to hunt and then resting with his crop almost bursting while the remnants of his kill draped the twigs and branches beneath. Tomorrow and tomorrow, he would enjoy the short life of a free-born, free-flying hawk. He would skim the hedge-tops and sweep out over the wood, and on the pasture flocks of starlings would stop toddling across the grass in search of insects when, next winter, he hunted with his eye turned orange and his plumage completely moulted.

After I had hung up the small hawk's leash, swivel and jesses and put away the soft glove which I had never really needed once his initial fear of me had declined, I stowed away the perches. I was almost at the end of the thing. I had known two birds of prey. But then a friend telephoned me to ask if I could take over and keep two lanner falcons. Lanners are sturdy, solid, coarse-footed and calm birds compared with the hawk kind. They are also very handsome. The pair were male and female. The male was less amenable to handling than the female. Both needed a great deal more feeding than the small hawk but then, since I was neither going to hunt them

nor train them to fly to my fist, I could fill their crops well
with jackdaw or pigeon, which I could shoot around
my own little wood and put them out to 'weather' and
take them in at night. Once again, however, I became
deeply attached to these two falcons. There was something about the darkness of the eye that made their movements and intentions unpredictable and I had to study
them closer than I had studied the hawks. Day after day,
however, they came to know me better and when I
approached them tethered on their blocks they would
fly up to my glove. I would find a small piece of meat for
them. Every time I passed they turned their heads and
watched me intently. They had this capacity to follow
someone walking behind them that almost convinced an
observer that their heads turned through 360 degrees.

After a month or so I took them back to their owner and
cleaned up the hawk hut. I was done with it all, I told
myself. I loved hawks and falcons but I wasn't a falconer.
That very day a young man arrived at my door saying
that he had heard that I kept hawks. News of this kind
gets about. An old lady in one of the houses in the town
down below actually complained that 'my' hawks were
killing small birds in her garden. It seemed that the little
musket had been hunting close to the door! I confessed
that I had some slight acquaintance with hawks and
falcons but said I was a novice and in fact I had decided
to keep no more tethered birds. The young man was
downcast. He didn't need my advice. He didn't want to
obtain a hawk. He wanted to pass one on to someone
who knew how to feed a bird and would care for it.
I weakened and accepted his falcon, paying a nominal
sum for it and installing it in the hawk hut. The bird was
a lagger or lugger falcon, as it is sometimes called. It was
smaller than the lanner but not unlike them. I soon had
it on my glove for it had already been manned. We
walked abroad. I fed it well. It left my fist and came back
to me. I didn't starve it to bring it into hunting fettle.

I only weighed it when I suspected that it was suffering from some infection. Falcons can be turned into pets. They lose their dignity and cease to have the keen fierce look of the bird of prey. A lagger can look rather like a parrot when this happens. I had almost entrapped myself again but I was no falconer, merely a keeper of a falcon, reducing it to the equivalent of a lap-dog. I became depressed about this and determined never to keep another hawk of any kind.

By some chance my disenchantment was advertised among a circle of acquaintances and one day a detective inspector arrived to enquire if I would sell him my falcon. It seemed that when he wasn't hunting thieves he hunted with hawks. I put the lagger on his fist, accepted exactly the sum I had given for the bird, and closed the door of the hawk hut for good. The sum of my experience was considerable. I would not be without it. I know things about birds of prey I would never otherwise have known. I have a much better understanding of ecology and sentimentalist though I may admit to being, I know sentimentality to be a kind of world blindness, a refusal to accept things as they really are.

4

A-Hunting I did Go

WITHOUT doubt I was born wild, the way a fox or a hawk is wild. Such efforts as those who were responsible for my upbringing made by way of making me a quiet, civilised being were no more than partially successful. I was excited by the chase. It began with the excitement of following a dog on the trail of a stackyard rat and continued when I led that well-balanced, working dog away from its proper course and took it hunting in the fields beyond. Away we went, over the gorse hillocks and through the woods, along the hedges and among the rushes. Poor dog, being no use for his work when we were finally parted, and being much wilder and savage on account of his hunting freedom, he was executed. A shotgun blast put him down, poor fellow. I never forgot him. His spirit and mine still thread through the tall bracken on the scent of a pheasant and I whoop encouragement when our quarry breaks cover a jump away from his snarling mouth. He was a Border collie, I hasten to explain. We corrupted each other. I recall his face better than the faces of many men I have met. We were kin to one another. His name was Tweed. His life was wild and short while he reverted to whatever hunting ancestry he had, and I joined him.

It was this excitement that drew me to the company

of some hill shepherds who, every weekend, spent their time hunting foxes with a terrier pack. Oh, it was a barbaric business. I confess to my vice with more than a little shame for it came upon me when the schoolmasters had long finished with me and I was free to choose. The outcome of it all was very different from what might be expected. I had no idea how it would change the course of my daily life and make me not a hunter but a shepherd. On Sunday mornings, long before the first chapel-goers were creaking along the village street in their best boots and shoes, I would meet the fox-hunting desperadoes. They had an old van into which they all bundled along with the terrier pack, spades, guns, a crowbar and other odds and ends of gear. It didn't matter that the van would only take six or seven in comfort. It carried ten or twelve if need be, and the smell of the earth was strong. The irrepressible terriers swarmed over bodies, snapped and snarled and growled, sniffed and sometimes burrowed down into the straw that made the floor less hard when we rocked and bounced and bumped on our way to the mountain. The expedition was a religious one, in a manner of speaking, for as surely as the faithful faced the rain or the snow to go to chapel, this company of fox-diggers went to the mountain. They took nothing in the way of food. They were prepared to climb uphill for an hour and run down a long, sliding scree to do the same thing again in the next valley. The war-scarred Jack Russells and Border terriers ran with them. With their ancient guns and tattered, tied-at-the-waist coats they looked like tribesmen. I would swear that their boots had rocker soles and not flat soles so that they could roll uphill and down with the same half-running strides. Three or four of them were shepherds or the sons of owners of mountain flocks. The rest were addicts of the drug that is in mountain air, in the cold wind that whispers through giant rocks, the scent of burned heather and wet moss.

For my part I was almost always at the tail-end of the

uphill file although I sometimes ran a scree at such speed that I could believe I could hold my own with any of them. More often than not I came to the cluster of boulders or crags when the terriers had marked and gone below. By this time the watchers would be spread out with their old guns and the hunters would be there in the middle of it all, peering down into the dark recesses among the rocks, listening to the yelps of terriers away down below or simply waiting for the leader of the pack to emerge again with lesser dogs and bitches following. I was conscious of being something of an outsider on these occasions. I was aware that some things that might have been done when I wasn't there were now not done in case I frowned upon them, things that were too barbaric except for initiated barbarians. I never shot but one fox in all my life and that one had a gin trap on his leg. My companions suspected that if a fox bolted I would let him go. Somehow there were always guns a little to my left or right as a precaution against my wilting under fire. A fox that eluded the ferocious terrier pack or fought his way out deserved to run, I said, but they were hill shepherds and blamed the fox for the death of every lamb, even if the keep on the mountain was barely enough to allow the ewe to survive let alone feed her lamb. I loved to see the fox run. I understood how well his fat brush balanced him when he jumped from one great slab of rock to another. He carried himself so well heading into the wind with his tail rippling. I ran with the fox and hunted with the pack. There was nothing orgiastic about a kill. It was, in fact, an anticlimax and worse, a sad thing, a tragedy.

Once, peering down between slabs of slate I saw the fox backed into a corner by three snarling terriers who rushed at him so often and did such fearful damage that his nose was ripped bare to the bone. I couldn't protest. I couldn't get the pack out of that narrow slot any more than their owners could. When one or two emerged and

someone attempted to grab them they reacted like tigers.
I doubt whether anyone who hasn't hunted with terriers
can appreciate the ferocity of the pack. They cease to be
individual animals. Four or five small, rough-coated,
snorting terriers weighing perhaps eight or ten pounds
apiece become collectively more dangerous than a bear.
Such creatures have been known to savage a child.
Indeed, not so long ago, a pack killed a toddler and no
one could make them hear or, if they heard, obey or
respond to blows. The murder of the fox, on the occasions
when kills were made, was once counterbalanced when the
terriers went down and met, instead of a fox, an old
badger who had taken to the hills. What mutilation the
pack suffered on that outing! Two or three refused to go
below again. The badger had imprinted terror upon them
and they were, in the words of their owners, useless for
anything but chewing on old bones.

The shepherd's hatred of the fox arises from the
economy of sheep-breeding between upland meadows
and mountain. The losses are often heavy. The grass is
rarely sufficient. Lambs that are sickly fall to the waiting
crows. The buzzard picks the rib bones. The fox comes
to grind them. A vixen makes a quick foray and parts a
ewe from twin lambs by running at one and then at the
other until they are separated. This achieved, she lures
the ewe to advance and attack her and then whips past
her, kills, and makes off with the lamb. This kind of thing
has been witnessed by the hill shepherd. His frustrations
in general come to focus when he sees the fox or discovers
the earth. I was studying the shepherd at close range at
this time for I was writing a book about his life. I knew
how he walked the hill and how he turned his face away
from the stinging winter hail, but I had to know what he
thought about creatures other than sheep. The hill
shepherd's thoughts are mostly concerned with predators
on the fringes of his flock. The fox is easier located and
dealt with than the crow.

When I gave up following the terrier pack it wasn't because I was suffering from cramp and loss of breath. I had become hardened to ridge-running and climbing over endless plateaux to reach new escarpments and steeper screes, but I had had enough of the business. Being a John Peel was one thing, but the ambush and the hole-and-corner murder were more than I could stomach. I was no bounty hunter. The tail of a fox might bring a reward but I would never hold it in my hand, let alone apply for it. I had, however, a hankering to keep sheep. Would it not be a good thing to have some sheep of my own to keep down the grass and please me when I looked out of my bedroom window? I could hardly resist the dream. In fact, in less than a week I had been in touch with one of those hill shepherds and he had promised to bring me my flock, six well-grown lambs from the mountain flock he tended. Some things are written and there is no escaping them. I little knew what I was doing when I set about railing off the old orchard so that my sheep could have temporary quarters there while I did something of the sort with the larger area of land on the slope beyond the cottage. I might not be able to pose with a crook while I counted my sheep, for it doesn't take long to count six and recheck, even twice or three times, but I would be doing something that ran in the family, being a husbandman, providing meat for my table! I had bought a deep freeze. The obvious thing to do was to kill off the lambs in due course and deep-freeze the cuts of meat. I saw myself with an almost endless supply of home-fattened lamb, chops by the dozen, legs and shoulders, livers and hearts. I would skin my sheep and cure the skins. I even went off and found an old friend who had served his time at the butcher's trade and could tell me not only how to skin a lamb, but how to joint it. I was counting my chickens before they were hatched!

When the telephone rang to say that my small flock

was on its way I was excited. I could hardly wait for the lambs to arrive. The van trundled up the lane one dark night in November and with the help of my friends I half-carried each lamb (feet tied with baler twine) to the barricades of the old orchard, popped each lamb over and let it amble off into the darkness once the twine was cut. It all took no more than twenty minutes and I was a shepherd in my own right. We drank a glass of whisky and toasted one another. The professionals departed. I stood a while and then went out to the orchard with the handlamp to count my sheep for the first time. I counted the twelve gleaming eyes of lambs in darkness and went to bed to the sound of their occasional bleating.

Could I have ever been so unobservant as to think that sheep eat fresh grass and ruminate upon it? Welsh mountain sheep are perverse creatures and eat grass only when there is nothing else! First they eat the bark from trees and the ivy from walls. Above all else they will eat ivy. I thought of the sometime popular tune about little lambs eating ivy. My shaggy sheep looked far from little and they certainly weren't innocent. In daylight they galloped off in a panic the moment they saw me, going round and round the old orchard, which has a steep slope, as fast as their short, strong legs would carry them. They didn't stop to be numbered. Only a high-speed shutter could have caught them in action and allowed them to be counted. The hammering of their sharp hooves chopped the orchard grass to a turfy tilth in no time. In the night they stood still, high on their hind legs, eating the bark of the trees. Did they not recognise me as their shepherd? Were they all mad, like Gadarene swine? I was dismayed. I had had a vision of myself stepping into the orchard that morning and being the centre of a pastoral scene. I had a Sunday school picture of myself and a text in mind—The Good Shepherd loveth his flock. All I should have needed was a lamb to cradle in my arms! I have often been told that I look a little like John the Baptist.

I am a man of the wilderness. My background is the cry of the bird of the mountain, the sound of the flute and peace while the slow-moving shadow of the cloud passes over the green hill. All this was in absurd contrast to reality. The lambs wanted away. They had never been so confined except perhaps when their mothers were in the shearing pens or being dipped for scab. I didn't look like a shepherd, but more like a heavily disguised butcher perhaps and a lamb's path leads but to the butcher's slab.

I went off and put the finishing touches to the fence of the little orchard and the wych-elm hedge of what had at one time been the kitchen garden. Now I only had the problem of getting the sheep from one part of the small 'estate' to the other. All I needed to do, I told myself, was to open the barrier on the old orchard and go to the far end whereupon my circus of rushing sheep would dash out, pass along the side of the greenhouse, head for the court and the cottage, see no outlet there, and turn sharply to their left, up the path and along to the little orchard which was well-fenced from the wood behind. I did this. My flock performed like Roman horses in the arena and charged out, but they didn't go to the little orchard. They took the side track, straight uphill to the cliff. They were, after all, mountain sheep and they preferred to run uphill. I swear that their forelegs are slightly shorter in proportion to those of ordinary breeds. Away they rushed at top-speed, everyone determined to be first to the top, regardless of the long arms of blackberry and the thorns of rose and haw. I set out after them, calling my younger son to come and play sheepdog, if his breath would hold out long enough for us to cut off the Gadarene sheep before they jumped down over the cliff which comprises the greater part of our four acres.

It takes a wily dog to round up sheep. Two frantic would-be shepherds don't make one half-useful sheepdog.

The six lambs tore away first to the left through a forest of gorse and blackthorn, and then to the right through a gap in a wall and away to the boundary at the top of the pine wood. We followed and they tore downhill at the same high speed. We went down and they circum-navigated us and rushed uphill. Their sides heaved. Our tongues hung out. I felt the image of myself as a shepherd was already besmirched, tarnished, even pathetic. By a subterfuge we got them going downhill again towards the little orchard and the pigeon house which is built into the step of the land at the far corner. The sheep rushed through the holly and thorns, dodged and darted and one by one rushed straight onto the roof of the pigeon house to jump the full seven feet down into the concrete yard of what was once a piggery! Ordinary sheep would have lain there, their forelegs broken and their life blood ebbing away, but not my flock. They seemed to be made of rubber and elastic for no sooner did one land, sprawl though it might, than it was up and off at the same speed. One thing had been achieved. We had the flock in the enclosure. We had run several pounds' live weight off each one, and probably half a stone off myself. I had lost my enthusiasm. The sheep had lost all appetite for they stood together, as far from me as they could get, watching me with wild eyes. I went indoors and with as much breath-control as I could manage said, 'Well, that's it. They're safely closed in in the kitchen garden. The place is almost knee-deep in lush green grass, despite the month of the year. All we need to do is wait for them to fatten up.'

The following day I went and bought a professional's skinning knife and spent some time making little sketches of the cuts of lamb: saddle, neck, ribs, loin, etc., etc. I looked out at my flock. They wandered about aimlessly. I little thought that they were looking for a way out and had no intention of waiting to have their throats cut, or the knife inserted in the skilful manner I had been shown

by my instructor. I thought about it. My enthusiasm for
turning those restless, frightened, disoriented creatures
into meat for my table began to wane from that moment.
I would hate them and love them in turn from this day
on, but I wouldn't have the stomach for killing. The
flock-leader, for every group of sheep will produce one
animal that leads the way in whatever nonsense they get
up to, explored the bushes and hanks of wire netting
which I had stuffed into holes in the somewhat open-
growing wych-elm hedge. He found a way as he must have
known he would. I could only be thankful that when I
counted my flock and discovered that I had lost a sixth
of its number, the others hadn't followed suit. The
escaper hadn't been content to go like a battering ram
through a hole in the stalks and stems of the wych elms
and drop down the sheer side of a five-foot limestone
wall but he had bulldozed his way through a blackthorn
thicket close enough to daunt an elephant and pushed on
into my neighbour's field! There he was, out there in the
green open space in the middle of a flock of sixty wintering
sheep. The sixty had blue marks. My own had a red
mark on the rump as well as the ear-marks of the flock
from which he had come.

The form in such a case is to go to one's neighbour,
express regret that animals have strayed, and ask permission to cut the strays out of his flock. This can be
done with a couple of good sheepdogs and some hurdles.
Anyone who has seen a sheepdog trial knows how simply
it can be done—with one or two sheepdogs. I had none.
One good thing about it, I noticed, was that my neighbour
was feeding those wintering sheep. He needed to. His
pasture was like an old worn carpet. I went to him and he
laughed. A stray? Well, unless I was in a hurry, I could
leave the stray where it was. It would come to no harm.
In due course he would cut it out and deliver it back to
me in his truck. I agreed. A sixth of my worry was being
taken care of. I regretted the fact that by losing a sixth

I had that much less claim of being a flockmaster. I went back and closed the gap and counted my flock again. They had eaten a little bark off the young fruit trees. I was anxious about that. Tomorrow I would cut down some ivy from the walls, and while they were eating the ivy, I would put wire cages round my young and valuable trees. I cut the ivy, but the flock were not at peace. They didn't stop to eat while I caged the fruit trees but ran into this corner and that corner every time I turned my head. I knew deep in my heart that the mountain sheep were suffering from a Welsh complaint—*hiraeth*—a longing for the place from which they had come. Not only Welshmen suffer these awful pangs of something like homesickness, but little Welsh mountain sheep have it and suffer anguish until they are back on the mountain. It is wellknown among the shepherds that mountain sheep are 'homers' just like racing pigeons. My sheep would have been away, across the estuary and back to their mountain but for my daily inspection of the defences and finally, an acute change in the weather. Snow came. What more did I need to increase my anxieties and double my labour, for now I had to cut and carry food to the flock. My neighbour sold me a couple of bales of hay but mountain sheep disdain hay until they are about to fall off their legs. It is the last thing they will eat. The hay remained untouched. My neighbour said he had feared it would be so. If my sheep starved until they ate the hay they would never fatten enough to be fit for the deep freeze or the market.

I began to cut ivy and deliver it in sackfuls to them. They ate all I could carry. We had tons of ivy, but cutting it when it is snow-laden and frozen is a wearying task. I performed it until I saw that I was no more than a sort of harvester of the walls and the trees of the wood, occupied for five hours cutting what the sheep could devour in half an hour. It struck me that I must do as the good husbandman did, and buy food at the depot. I went off and consulted the salesman. Lamb pencils, you want, he said. I bought a couple of sacks. The sheep loved them. They gobbled them down so fast that they reminded me of the threshing machine consuming sheaves. They ate ivy between times. They kicked the snow and ate the lank, now dead, grass. They began to trot towards me making me feel, at long last, that I was the good shepherd and they were my flock. No creature looks more pathetic than a hungry sheep. Its big eyes are liquid. It sniffs the air delicately. It waits but knows not why. It trots behind the man who feeds it like a faithful dog. He begins to represent food and the flock will then come any distance to be fed. I began to get so deeply attached to the sheep that I couldn't bear the thought of them being out on the frozen slope at night. I constructed a small shelter for them and stopped the draughts with handfuls of the hay they had refused to eat. They crowded into the shelter because I put food in there but they 'roosted' on the bare slope. There they left thawed-out, brown patches when they arose and came up to the gate to wait for me in the morning. I had come to know sheep at last. I knew the smell of them, the stupidity of them, their agility, for they could take off and sail through the air in horizontal flight for four or five times their own length!

Day after day I toiled at shepherding. My lost sheep trotted with my neighbour's flock and I had half a mind to make a hole in the hedge and gain a day or two's respite while the other five integrated with his large flock. This, many a Welsh shepherd has been known to do, when feed is hard to come by and the pasture eaten bare, but I was an amateur and an amateur is in the business for the love of it. I had to soldier on until the grass grew again. I hadn't really noticed that although the grass grows in spring its growth rate is impossible to detect except with instruments, microscopes. It takes a long, long time to grow after sheep have eaten down to the

Ian Niall and Lanner Falcon   (*Seán Hagerty*)

Ian Niall's son with a pet buzzard on a bicycle borrowed
for the bird's benefit   (*Country Life*)

View from the tower—cottage among the pines bottom right   (*Country Li*

Author on the path from the long greenhouse into the wood

(Country Life)

Author fishing a mountain lake   *(Country Life)*

Feeding the hens at Tan-yr-Allt Cottage

(*Seán Hage*

Some of the birds around the house   (*Seán Hagerty*)

The cockerel that might have been a phantom   (*Seán Hagerty*)

The trap in which Ian Niall caught an escapee bantam
16 days after it had flown away   (*Seán Hagerty*)

Special beehive, designed and built by Ian Niall

(*Seán Hagerty*)

The beehives in the old orchard   (*Seán Hagerty*)

Author with very special bantam   (*Seán Hagerty*)

roots. My sheep had done that and more. They had become accustomed to eating lamb pencils and lamb pencils were costly. I counted the heads, six sheep for which I had paid a very small sum, eighteen pounds altogether, a bargain price for lambs. I counted the cost of the food I had bought. I dared not count the cost of my labour, accord myself a shilling or two for the cold and wet I had suffered, the backache, the misery. Then, too, there was the damage to the fruit trees. I could see that some of my three-year-old apple trees which had newly started to bear fruit were badly maimed. They would carry the scars of my shepherding days as long as they grew.

The butcher and I met once a week. Word had got round that I was in business and had become my own provider. Lambs, was I managing to fatten them? He wasn't able to fatten his own lambs. I suppose he thought to demoralise me. My lambs looked fat, I said. They were well-fed. Any time he cared to come and handle them he could do so. I had farming blood in my veins. I knew about sheep instinctively even though the Welsh breed baffled me at times. The butcher beamed at me. I think he felt that the experience was ageing me. I would soon come to my senses. There was no profit in sheep without the subsidy, he said. I was secretly depressed, but the brighter light of spring helped to improve my frame of mind. My neighbour cut out the stray and brought it back. He bundled it very expertly over the side of his truck and delivered it into my arms. He said it wasn't fat but it wasn't skin and bone. I offered some lamb pencils in return for the food my stray had taken at his trough but he laughed and waved my offer aside. We were both flockmasters, after all. So few people knew about sheep. Most thought lamb was too expensive and the shepherd's life was like a poet's, nothing but day-dreams and the scent of meadows.

With every day that passed now I brooded over my

flock. I couldn't kill them. I could hardly bear the thought
of the butcher having them. I looked more often into
their foolish, woolly-polled faces and felt a deep compassion for them. Other sheep were not my sheep. I
didn't know them and therefore I wasn't involved in their
lives or in control of their destiny but what was the
alternative? It seemed I must become reconciled to the
ruining of a small orchard that had been my pride and
joy when I planted it, for my 'lambs' were now well-
trained in walking on their back legs and balancing for
minutes on end while they browsed on the buds of the
trees. I would have to sell them into the hands of the
Philistines but I didn't know a Philistine who would buy
them. I moved them out of the little orchard into the old
one, thinking that they would do less damage there. They
might even ring-bark the old trees and actually make them
produce a little fruit. This was nonsense, of course. My
sheep did eat all the young shoots of the old trees and
stood waiting for more ivy and more helpings of lamb
pencils. They made the grass of the old orchard disappear
in no time and the slope became dangerous when it
rained, for now they had consolidated the soil and the
rain turned the skin of the hard ground into a slime of
mud upon which I slipped and slid as I went down to
remove the branches and stalks of the ivy I had tipped
wholesale down among the fruit trees.

There never was a shepherd with so much on his mind.
I couldn't live with and look after six sheep for the rest
of my life. I put out feelers with the butcher again. He
enjoyed himself a little, asking me if I wanted my sheep
killed and delivered, killed and sold in his shop or taken
away and preserved as monuments to my shepherding
phase? I shuddered to think of any of these things. Long
ago a hill shepherd had assured me that he knew the face
of every sheep he owned. Every one of his flock was as
easily recognised as his own relatives or immediate circle
of acquaintances. I had thought this nonsense but now

I knew that if I looked at my six sheep they were not identical. With a sense of horror I knew each one, the crafty one, the fool, the nervous one and the boldest of them. They too, knew me and I even began to see my expression reflected in their foolish eyes. None of this helped me at all. The butcher recognised me for the sort of man who should never own an animal he intends to eat. There were people who wouldn't eat meat, denying that man is either a carnivorous or predatory creature. Good luck to them. There are many more hypocrites who are sentimental about particular animals and prefer not to know that a steak is part of a bullock. Garnished with this and that, nestling in onions or surrounded by mushrooms or almost floating in a cream sauce laced with brandy, a steak is a long, long way from the soft expression on the face of a Jersey cow. This is where I stood, among those who prefer to have their killing done for them and to pretend that there isn't a trace of blood seeping into the sauce.

It was getting on towards Easter. The grass diminished before it had started to grow. I went to the depot again and again. They began to know me there. I flushed when they asked me how my sheep had wintered for they took me for some sort of a flockmaster, albeit a dilettante one. I looked at the hills and said it would be a while before the grass came. They talked about the price of lamb. Already some of the valley flocks had lambs that were half ready for market. I took my bags of pencils and drove home to look again at the havoc in the old orchard and the bareness of the walls and the cliff ledges where I had harvested the ivy until there was hardly a leaf to be had. One day I met my hill shepherd friend. He asked about the flock I had bought from him. No, he didn't want them back. They would by now be broken of their longing for their native hill. They wouldn't fetch the best price in the market and there wouldn't be a profit in it for either of us. He was very honest. He had no compassion for my pet sheep or for me in my mental torment. I would look at them and swear that never again if I lived to be a hundred would I keep sheep. A man must know a great deal more about himself than I did before he embarks upon such a venture. Somewhere along the way I had lost the practical, peasant outlook that should have been ingrained in my being. I had become a sentimentalist with a vengeance and the only solution I could find was in the fact that the weakness had been in my blood, for I remembered the weeping of my aunts when a favourite pig was being butchered. They had cried like bereaved children, burying their faces in their aprons while the poor pig shrieked as the man with the killing knife advanced upon him.

What will you do? asked my wife. I looked away out to the horizon beyond the north shore and said I would come to it. I would face up to what must be done and the sheep would go to be butchered. We wouldn't eat any of the meat.

5

The Innocent Lamb

BRAVE talk comes easiest to the lips of cowards. I looked
at the flock and walked away from them, putting them
from my mind as far as I was able when each day I had
to see that they were fed. I had other things to think
about. One of the delights of spring for me is the anticipation of my first expedition to fish. I dream about fishing
in the winter. The dream is always better than the reality,
but in the spring I look up at the hills and wonder when
the snow cap will melt on the highest peaks and the last
snow blots diminish from the depressions on the north-
eastern slopes. When the snow goes, the lakes begin to
get just a little warmer. The trout come higher in the
water in the first days of spring sunshine, occasionally
making a ring as they take a fly or bulge the surface for
a nymph about to hatch. I take myself to the hills every
spring to clear the cobwebs from my mind, to see the
bleached grass recovering from the snow that covered it
for days or even weeks on end, and I love to hear the
curlews crying on the upland moors as they search for
nesting places.

There was now only one thing wrong with this annual
escape of mine. At the same time as the hills begin to lose
their snow peaks the shepherds begin to assemble their
flocks. They won't pay the valley pasture fee a day longer

than they need. In any case, the contract is generally limited and the valley pastures, worn bare, must have a chance to recover. On the mountain there are always a few wintering sheep, old wethers that can live where nothing else could survive but the hill fox. The newly brought-up flocks drive these old, shaggy, dirty grey sheep still farther up the slopes and into the remote cwms. Wherever I went I was reminded of my own mollycoddled sheep. I could hear the distant bleating of the flocks. I could see them dotting the stretches of dead bracken and heather and places where some of the old growth was being burned off by the graziers to provide better pasture for their flocks in another spring. My trouble was my paternal involvement with sheep much hardier than I could believe them to be. No shepherd would ever have shown so much concern for them as I had done and they would have thriven despite what I would have called neglect.

I fished and thought about it all. Sheep like mine were working their way along cliff ledges and browsing on short fine herbage two or three hundred feet above the water. Now and again one of them lost its balance and slipped on the fine grass to come crashing down, head over heels, striking the protruding crags to plunge into the water. Once, one of these ewes landed only a few feet away from me. Some of the small stones it brought with it fell about my head and one large boulder, bouncing on another on the shore, left a sort of gunpowder odour in the air. The casualties are continual and a part of the price of keeping a mountain flock on grazing that costs very little in rent. The shepherds plod up the mountain and scan the far ridges for their own sheep, sending their dogs out to bring down those suspected of having some ailment like foot rot or maggot. The whole business is hard, cool and to a pattern that began perhaps on the pastures of the Middle East or the mountains of India, except that those long-ago flockmasters stayed with their charges day and night, defending their sheep from the attacks of wolves or other predators.

I could smile at my folly while I fished and enjoyed the solitude, but every now and then I was reminded of my sheep by the bleating that punctuated the great silence. The decision wasn't urgent. It wasn't being forced upon me. It nagged in my mind the way getting a garden plot ready for planting nags in the mind of a conscientious gardener. I came home from my fishing and looked at my sheep. They couldn't very well go back to the mountain. The shepherds didn't want more sheep. They had all they needed. And then it was the Easter holiday. People react to Easter in much the same way as they react to New Year. Easter marks the spring whether it comes early or late, and if the weather is at all fine people are off, plodding the lanes and the footpaths looking for catkins or some small flower, like the wild snowdrop, that will confirm that the season really has changed. I heard the occasional group of people going up the lane and on over the stile. I looked at the first daffodil opening on the slope where the pine trees grow. I heard my sheep bleating but I was less depressed. Most of us live upon our recollection of happiness or misery and I could remember my mother taking me to roll a dyed, hard-boiled egg down a grassy slope at Easter. I remember all Easters as bright and cool with a radiant sun high in the sky. It never rained and the sky was never dark. It was like that on Easter Monday. I stood at the top corner of the old orchard and smiled as I listened to a boy, hidden from me by the ten-foot limestone wall, standing in the lane and imitating a bleating lamb. He did it so well that I was amused. His ear must be very good, I told myself. He could have fooled a ewe, and then, as the bleating went on and on I found it tiresome. I couldn't imagine why the boy took such pleasure in monotony and I half thought of calling out to him and telling him to go away. It was a minute or two before I

saw what I had been looking at, but when I understood
I gaped. Down at the foot of the wall was a white object,
hardly bigger than a ladies' handbag. It moved and the
bleating continued. My flock had somehow increased
from six to seven! A lamb had been born, but was this
possible since my sheep had come to me as lambs, albeit
well-grown lambs?

I scrambled down through the trees and examined
the lamb. One of my six sheep detached itself from the
others and took a tentative step in my direction. Possible
or not, I had an Easter lamb. The family must hear about
it! I rushed away to the cottage to break the news. The
five sheep made their usual mad dash round and round.
The mother of the lamb went down to her offspring.
I only looked back once to make sure I hadn't been
dreaming.

'I have another lamb!' I said.

No one understood at first. Did I mean that someone
else's sheep had strayed onto our ground? It wouldn't
have been the first time. Once I had had sixty-five intruders. Seeing is believing, they say. I invited the unbelievers
to see for themselves and they came out and saw the ewe
and her lamb. The small thing, fashioned, it seemed, from
matchwood and cotton wool, tottered away after its
mother. A strong breeze would have blown it over. It
looked like a crochet-work, limp bag. Its coat was curly
white astrakhan. It would never survive! This is one of the
things about the mountain lamb that people who know
nothing about it are liable to think. The creature is so
unco-ordinated in its movements, so fragile, that when
it moves it seems to be on the verge of collapse. Its legs
splay, its back bends, its head wobbles and it looks the
most helpless creature that was ever brought into the
world, but within that frame there are thongs or sinews
strong as a whiplash. The sprawling and staggering are
an illusion or something calculated to invoke pity in the
heart of sentimental onlookers. The animal is as hard to

kill as the peasant who bred it. It will stand on the lea side of its mother when the snow freezes on her fleece. It will articulate its bag of bones over the roughest ground and follow wherever its mother leads. Barring accident, or congenital weakness, it will prove itself a born survivor!

My Easter Monday lamb filled me with delight for at least an hour. It was probably the first lamb ever born on this piece of ground. It had come naturally, as a good healthy lamb will, and it was already able to follow and suckle its mother who was none the worse for having given birth on a cold night. What now, however, about the butcher and my plans to be done with sheep once and for all? The ewe must be given the chance to rear her lamb. The lamb must be fattened. I had a feeling that it might be with us for a long time. Could I not keep just the ewe and her lamb and let the butcher have the others?

My shepherd friend was very amused about the lamb. He had had no idea that this would happen. Very occasionally late lambs proved fertile and lambed in the following spring or early summer. Usually he separated the lambs from the main flock so that they were properly matured before they were bred from. No, he said, he hardly thought I needed to send for the vet and have the lamb injected for liver fluke. One day, by the sound of it, we would meet in the market, each with a thousand sheep to sell! I laughed at that and telephoned the butcher. Yes, he would come and take the five lambs I had 'wintered'. Mind you, they would have to be worth buying. It hadn't been a very good winter for fattening sheep. His own flock was in no very great condition.

In the meantime I worked hard to provide the sheep with more food than ever. I poured lamb pencils into the trough, deciding that the ewe with the lamb needed more than her share of food since she had to feed her offspring. I carried and poured and carried and poured and the sheep bolted down all I put before them. The butcher telephoned to say that he would come after he had been to market on Monday and I immediately began to dread the moment. The sheep had walked at my heels like trained dogs. They had looked me in the face and I had understood their trust. Now, it seemed, they read a message in my eyes. Perhaps a man's intentions are communicated to animals. I have often felt that mine were. The sheep sensed that something was going to happen that evening when the butcher and his helpers arrived. The smell of blood and animal fat is in a butcher's clothes and however he approaches the sheep or bullock the poor creature knows him for what he is. My sheep never galloped round the orchard at such speed. It was hard to separate the ewe with her lamb from the five that were to go away, but at last this was achieved and the ewe and lamb were railed off in a corner.

'Now,' said the butcher, 'We won't be long getting the rest!'

But the butcher was over-optimistic. Railing off the ewe and her lamb had taken some time. The last crow had gone to roost in the wood. The chattering blackbirds had given up calling. It was almost night and the ground of the little orchard was moist. The butcher and his helpers slipped and skidded on the slope. The sheep proved more elusive than I had ever known them to be. Occasionally, flashing a torch to discover where they were grouped, I came upon their frightened faces and saw the glitter of their eyes in the beam of the torch. The butcher's men were black, wild creatures. I was sickened by the whole business. The first of the sheep was caught as it tried to dash past an ambush at the top of the slope, hauled onto its back legs and 'walked' to the barrier. It took a few minutes to get it away to the van. I loitered at a distance, hearing the shouting and the cursing, the drumming of feet and the occasional bleating of the frightened animals. I had brought it all upon myself, of course. The butchers were butchers and lambs were lambs. What a slaughterhouse was like I knew from childhood, but I had chosen to dream my way through the world. The second, and then the third and fourth sheep, went down the steps to the van, each strangely submissive and resigned to its fate when the time came. I imagined a man going to the gallows behaving in just the same way. The last of the five had more room and there was a greater desperation in him, for he had the three butchers on their knees and colliding with one another several times. There was talk of leaving him for another day. I would have agreed willingly but at that moment the unfortunate sheep slipped and was pounced upon. In a minute he was being marched off on his hindlegs, urged along by the knees of the man who had captured him.

'We could all do with a nice pint of beer!' said the butcher.

I agreed, but I wanted to be alone. I was depressed and had had enough of the smell of sheep and blood and mutton fat. I took the money in my hand and didn't count it. Thirty pieces of silver or thirty grubby pound notes that had changed hands all day in the market. It didn't make much difference. I knew how Judas felt. The foolish sheep had shown me as much trust as I had earned. They had followed me in their innocence and I had plotted their end with the butcher. From the little orchard I could hear the sound of the young lamb bleating. I went down and released the ewe and her offspring before I went indoors and poured myself a whisky.

The most depressing aspect of it all was that I still had that ewe and lamb to dispose of one way or another. I could put off the day by saying that the lamb would have to grow and fatten a little before it was ready and the ewe must be well taken care of in order to feed the lamb. I could let them both settle down, but I would have to work and look after them for as long as I lacked the courage to make the decision. A friend telephoned me to say that he had been offered some very special lamb and he had been told that I had reared it. I sighed and said I had. Had I not said that I was going to stock the deep freeze with lamb and not sell it to the butcher? I agreed I had. Now, however, I had a different outlook. I had become so fond of my sheep that I couldn't bear the thought of eating them. The story went round our old village where the butcher has his business. It amused everyone. I took the precaution of ringing the butcher and changing our standing order (he had been instructed to send whatever meat he felt was the best at any particular time). We would have no lamb for a month and that would surely make certain that none of my own rearing came to the table. The butcher laughed. I knew the foolishness of it. So long as I hadn't looked an animal in the face I could eat its flesh. Meat on my plate was something quite divorced from a living creature.

The ewe and her lamb never quite recovered from the shock of that wild foray made by the butchers. They were nervous of me. I was careful not to become involved with the new lamb. I would harden my heart against them and never look the lamb in the face. It would remain imprinted with the image of a man bearing down upon it with a knife in his hand and a steel dangling from his belt, or something only a degree less horrifying. I wouldn't know this lamb. I knew its mother, however, and she knew me as the person who had come along the snow-trodden path to feed her and the others in the coldest winter for years. Now and again she stopped and stared at me and I knew it would be even harder than before to ring the butcher and ask him to come and take away what I called the last of my flock.

In the old orchard the grass began to recover. The apple blossom fell. The lamb grew bigger and suckled its mother less frequently. I didn't need to provide so much food. The fox I had dreaded didn't come down. The passing of days meant very little except that we came to high summer and ewe and lamb were browsing as high as they could reach up the trunks of the old apple trees. I went off and fished for seatrout. I saw the shepherds penning their flocks for the summer shearing, and the combings of fleeces that were piled high on lorries adorning the thorn trees through which the wool-gatherers drove their vehicles. Flocks of shorn sheep flowed back up over the hills like rivers running the wrong way. The bleating drowned the call of the late cuckoos, the occasional cry of the curlew and the small voice of the wheater and the pipit.

'What will you do with the last of your sheep?' they asked me. It was summer and the plum tree was laden with golden plums. In the shade of the weeping tree were the hollows in which my sheep had rested. I thought about the winter and the wind roaring through the wood.

'I must talk to the butcher again,' I said, 'but I think I can fatten them a little more. The shepherds won't be selling their lambs yet. They know when they are ready.'

This was a piece of nonsense. My two sheep were walking round the orchard. The shepherds' flocks were scaling the crags. The nagging that was my conscience finally became no longer tolerable. I picked up the telephone at last and asked the butcher to come and take them away. He agreed without hesitation. He knew I could fatten sheep. I wasn't in the least flattered. I knew I was unfit to keep sheep.

The second visit of the butcher was made at dusk as before. The ewe wasn't hard to catch. She bleated plaintively and her lamb answered as she was bundled off. The lamb was gathered up in the butcher's arms and removed at speed. I stood in the quietness of the orchard. An owl came and settled on one of the electricity poles. It seemed to bow its head to get a better view of me, the man who had lost his sheep. Once again I went back indoors and took a glass of whisky to soften the agony.

I sat for a long time examining my conscience and how things had come to pass. I had begun with a firm and healthy determination to rear, and fatten six lambs, kill them off one by one to stock the deep freeze. I had seen myself cutting into a succulent, stuffed and boned shoulder of lamb and having chops and liver all garnished with the most mouth-watering gravies or sauces. Along the way I had suffered a softening of the brain, lost sight of the fact that life and death are a cycle, endless, continual, everlasting. I slept on the result of my final self-examination. I had one more decision to make. In the morning I must make up my mind to ring the butcher and ask him to kill, skin and joint the lamb, reserving it entirely for the family. I would eat the lamb, enjoy its meat, have its fine curly skin cured, washed, brushed and combed to make a rug for my bedroom. Unless I did this I would never convince myself that I was a realist, capable of seeing that the world was as it was and not as I dreamed.

'Ah,' said the butcher, 'and quite right. You have reared a fine lamb there! It would be a pity to let it go over the counter to people who really don't know what it takes to produce such meat.'

At the end of the week the butcher's van trundled up to the cottage and one of the butchers got down and carried in the great basket of joints, legs, shoulders, ribs, best-end of neck, liver and heart, each portion neatly bagged in polythene. The skin was rolled and tied in a bundle. It looked a little messy and more like my lamb than the rest of the consignment. I put it in the potting shed and went off to study an old recipe for curing a lamb's skin which I had found in a book on taxidermy. The polythene parcels went into the deep freeze. The liver was cooked for lunch while I pegged the skin on a large board, scraped away the layer of fat and began to rub in the mixture of alum and saltpetre which would cure it and not make it too unpliable.

The scars of the shepherding enterprise were evident

as the leaves began to change colour. Every fruit tree
was barked. Gooseberry bushes that had been browsed
upon as they came into leaf would never bear fruit again.
The sheep had cut the fine soil and stones into screes.
Only the coarse herbage grew and things like dock and
ragwort. Sheep are fastidious about the sort of things they
will eat even when they are almost starving to death.
I met one of the shepherds when he was exercising a dog
on the mountain and he greeted me with great warmth.

'You did well with your sheep?' he asked.

'As well as could be expected,' I said and he laughed
for he had already marked me down as a sentimentalist.

'They are a lot of work,' he said. 'I often curse the day
my father put me to tending sheep. The work is hard.
The only good time is when you stand in the market
with the money in your hand and you know you haven't
made a loss.'

My experience had been different. I couldn't say that
I had known a good time except in the first few hours
when I counted the six sheep and felt that I was doing
something useful.

'You haven't thought of wintering a few more?' asked
the shepherd.

'I have resolved never to keep another sheep!' I said.
'I know all I want to know about sheep and a lot more
about myself.'

It took several weeks for the curing of the skin to be
effectively done and the fleece presentable as a rug
for the bedroom floor. Oddly enough, in this condition
it was no longer the lamb that had bleated at me on
Easter Monday. The meat that came out of the deep
freeze, because it had been properly killed, cooled and
frozen only once, was sweet and delicious to taste. I never
thought of it as the lamb born in the orchard. It was meat
on my plate. I had taken down the last of the barriers,
unstopped the holes in the wych-elm hedge and removed
all sign of my shepherding except a sort of lean-to I had

constructed between a wall and a tree so that the sheep could feed sheltered from the drifting snow.

My reputation as a dilettante shepherd had spread, however. Obviously I was a man interested in sheep and therefore in sheepdogs. I received an invitation to be president of a wellknown annual sheepdog trial. Alas, I was compelled to decline because of other engagements. I wrote and confessed that I was no kind of expert on sheepdogs. All my shepherding had been done personally, on foot and at a run. I had the greatest admiration for well-trained dogs, however. A man should never keep sheep without at least one dog or possibly two or three. The invitation came a second time but again I was otherwise engaged and had to decline. I wasn't really sorry. Someone might have persuaded me to buy a couple of Welsh collies and venture upon the business of training them and competing in trials. This would have meant getting more sheep and I was determined never to go back to being a shepherd, amateur or professional!

6

The Year of the Quail

THE year of the quail followed the year of the sheep. It wasn't that one can have more quail to the acre than sheep or even that it is easier to feed and look after a creature that weighs three ounces rather than one that grows to forty pounds. I was taken by the quail from the moment I first saw it. It wasn't the European quail that summers in some parts of southern England and was once a breeding bird in places as far apart as Galloway, Wales and Ireland, but the little Japanese quail. The Eastern bird is as dainty as a geisha, as plucky as a fighting cock. Indeed, Eastern people often gamble upon the cock quail in battle as keenly as the Mexicans crowd the gamecock main. I was fascinated by the tiny bird and both horrified and touched to discover it in the circumstances in which I first encountered it. The diminutive quails of Japan were in scaled-down battery cages, prisoners as much as battery hens encouraged to lay the maximum number of eggs by having the temperature of the room in which they lived thermostatically controlled. They, like the battery hens, were being fed a measured quantity of turkey crumbs and sipped water from little plastic bottles. The only difference between them and the battery hens was that each small cage included a cock bird and two hens. The presence of the cock ensured the continuation of the battery-bred strain. What saddened me wasn't so much the dull light and the over-warm room but the thought that these were birds that had never scratched an anthill or seen a small worm winding its way in the roots of the grass. They had never seen the sun and their plumage lacked lustre. I saw them free, in their natural state, rising above the grass and whirring away to alight where they wished or running like partridges along a furrow, wallowing in a dustbath and drinking from a spring.

All of this was a sentimental vision so far as the man in charge of the quails was concerned, for the quails were substitutes for the Guinea pig. They bred faster and not only the bird could be used for tests of one sort or another but the eggs, too, being fertile, allowed experiments to be made that would take a much longer time if the work had to be done on Guinea pigs. Rather hesitantly I asked if I might have a few quail. I could have a dozen if I wished and enough eggs to make an omelette or a salad! I was presented with a culling of quails in a minute and a dish of eggs. I hestitated again and explained that I had really hoped to be given a few live birds.

'Ah,' said the quail keeper, 'here you will run into a snag if you are thinking of breeding your own birds. You see, these are a battery generation. They are from a line of incubator-bred quail. They no longer have the capacity to sit upon and hatch their own eggs. The maternal instinct, you might say, has gone. The machine must do the job for them.'

I was even more depressed than before. The world we are making for ourselves and the creatures who happen to share it with us is one in which man takes upon himself the role of an omnipotent power. He isn't even conscious of himself in the role of God and to me this seems very dangerous, more dangerous than the key to the making of the most sophisticated kind of weapon for destroying man.

'I think,' I said, 'I can change the nature of the quails that have never seen daylight. I should like to try to breed them naturally.'

The suggestion brought a shrug. I felt that somehow I must be going against nature, trying to stop the inevitable change which is life and living. I went off with as many dead quail as would have made a feast for a gourmet, the eggs I had already been given, and a box containing a dozen live birds. Remember, I was told, these quail had been used to a warm room, quite draught-free. They were delicate things and the death rate could be high, considering the fact that they were all inbred. The whole business wasn't as simple as it looked.

The Japanese quail reminded me of the jack snipe. They were slight and there was nothing to them. They were ready to flutter up and take off and as I travelled with them in the car I could hear their wings beating against the lid of the cardboard box. I thought hard about the way I would bring them back to normal. I would introduce them to sandy soil on a greenhouse bed and give them a bushy branch of conifer or yew under which they could crouch and shelter. I would let them see the light of day and feel the breeze from the open door. They would pick and scratch and find small seeds which I would scatter in the earth for them and in a while they would become conditioned to a different environment and forget the wires of the cages into which they had been put the day they were transported from the electrically-heated brooder which adjoined their mother, the incubator.

'What next?' my friends asked me.

I explained another dream. The Japanese islands are comparable to the British Isles in temperature and rainfall. It seemed to me that the tiny Japanese quail could be acclimatised here and find suitable places in which to breed. I saw my own small acreage providing cover and all the insect food the Eastern quails might need. They would love the light soil, the straggling grass, the overhanging gorse and snowberry bushes. They would work their way among the jungles of blackthorn and bramble and elude their enemies by their speed, for all ground birds can run incredibly fast.

I had housed the birds in the long greenhouse, constructing a pen for them in a bed about twenty feet long by six feet wide about two feet above ground level. The pen consisted of large sheets of glass pushed into the soil. The roof was partly fine mesh wire and partly of glass. I cut yew and conifer and made a bower for them within the pen. I fashioned drinkers and feeding dishes but in the beginning I fed them the same diet as they had had from the time they were hatched, turkey crumbs. The little birds seemed bewildered. They ran this way and that, collided with the glass walls and flew up to hit the wire roof. The fine earth must have felt strange to their feet. At night they crowded together under the yew branch. Night had never fallen before. They had never been out of the light. I thought about that too as I closed the greenhouse door. What would they do if, in the darkness, a mouse or a vole came ploughing into their enclosure or some other predator tried to reach them. How many generations does it take to destroy the instinctive knowledge of danger and eliminate the way of self-preservation? I couldn't answer any of these questions. The little birds were more frightened of me than they had been of the laboratory assistant whose job it had been to change the water and collect their eggs. They had been laying as many eggs as the best strain of battery hen. The eggs were small, of course, but large enough to be boiled and eaten with a salad. They were coloured in a variety of markings and shades from brick-red to pale fawn, flecked and patterned most beautifully. My emancipated quail stopped laying immediately their feet touched the earth. The expert egg-producer could have told me why. The light and temperature change would have been enough to bring laying to an end. The shock of change and movement would put any bird off the lay for days, perhaps weeks, and these were no ordinary birds.

In the next two or three days I suffered my first casualty. A bird drowned in the drinking water and another caught a chill when I cooled the glass of the pen with a fine spray from the hose. The immediate reaction of the covey when I entered the greenhouse wasn't encouraging. They flew up in panic. They dashed themselves against the glass. They hid in cover and wouldn't come out again. They had also gone off their food. So much for my rehabilitation plan. I was making a poor show of playing God myself. In the hothouse atmosphere of the miniature battery house the little birds, knowing no other world, had been comparatively happy. All I seemed to be able to do for them was create eternal terror and they rose from the ground like small helicopters, whirring vertically, as rising quail will, until they struck the wire or glass above them. At this they would crash-land and dive into the dead foliage. So far they had taken no dust bath. I hadn't heard them piping and their freedom of movement in itself alarmed them. I began to think that soon I would have to do the humane thing and put an end to the experiment. The leopard can't change its spots in a generation of breeding. What had been done to these birds hadn't been done overnight. Environment is everything. We tend to forget this but it is a basic fact of life, and to change a background is not to solve the problem of the imprinted world which governs the behaviour of every creature in relation to its surroundings.

Eleven small quail, I told myself, to be returned to their prison which really wasn't a prison for them at all, to be quickly and humanely killed and given to someone who would baste them in a roasting dish, but certainly not to be set free to be caught by the first cat that stalked them. I already knew the responsibility of hacking back a hawk, introducing it gently to a world to which it properly belonged but in which it couldn't quite fend for itself on account of my foster-mothering it and finding it its daily ration. The poor quail wouldn't travel a hundred yards without meeting with disaster. The foraging stoats would come out of the hedge bottom, as they often did, and hunt them down in no time. The crow would swoop on them and kill them as neatly as he had once taken my father's pullets. If I gave them a few more days, I decided, they might begin to accept the facts of life in a new kind of pen. They might not be able to understand that they couldn't rush through a sheet of glass but I could take care of that by making the glass obscure. If I found a few small worms and dropped them into the pen perhaps the natural curiosity of the bird would induce it to investigate? I could only hope. I went off to dig for small worms but in the dry weather they were hard to find. I chopped up a few large worms but the quails didn't recognise the segments as food. I went down to a shop in the town and bought millet, teazle, linseed and scattered it on the earth of the floor of the pen hoping that the quail would discover that it was edible. They were drinking water. They had at least discovered that what was in an open dish was the same as they had sipped from the dripper in the battery cage. The cocks, I discovered, were beginning to fight. They squared up to one another and when I peeped in and they were unaware of my presence they hopped round and flew up and struck blows with their feet. Feathers were displaced and blood was drawn. Unless I did something about it there would surely be a fatal result.

At this stage I took stock of the birds and decided that I had three cocks. I had eight hens. A sheet of glass served as a partition and I divided the glass enclosure into three. Two cocks accompanied three hens each and one had only two females. The division didn't stop the cocks confronting one another or the hens flirting with cocks that couldn't reach them. The cocks threw themselves at the glass and fell down and got up again. In the meantime, given fewer turkey crumbs they began to scratch for seed. They began to find an insect and a seed. They occasionally fluffed up their feathers and took a dust bath but they remained terrified of my approach. The light was too bright. They had never lived in such a place. I was delighted, however, by their more natural behaviour. They were at least using legs and wings in a manner they had never used them before. They knew groundsel and lettuce leaves and if they still whirred up like helicopters, they also retreated into the cover I had provided in each enclosure. They picked and preened and then gradually they began to pipe the shrill piping note of the happy quail. I was delighted. I fussed and fretted over them, finding ants and beetles, small worms, grubs and even maggots, which they loved to bolt down. I found that the variety of mixed seeds put a sheen on their feathers. Every day they grew prettier. They also steadied down and discovered that some of my appearances meant special treats, a dish of pupae stolen from a newly opened ant colony, a few caterpillars delivered on the stalk of the plant they had been busy devouring. They liked a fine spray of water but I overdid it one day and suffered a third casualty after which I resolved to leave the birds to take a bath if they felt the need for it. The bath I provided was shallow enough to preclude any danger of the bathers drowning themselves. The diminutive quails, as handsome and colourful as any bird an artist ever painted, preferred to bathe in dust than to get their feathers wet. Time was passing. Summer was over. They hadn't laid an egg and I wasn't in the least concerned about that. I wanted them to lay in due course in spring or early summer when the light and temperature stimulated them to mate. If this happened perhaps the hens would become broody and incubate their eggs as their forebears would have done on the fields of Japan.

The winter was cold. I modified the living quarters of the birds. The cocks no longer fought. I constructed a sort of coop with a small entrance and a wooden floor. I insulated the whole thing as well as I could with polystyrene. I laid a thick blanket over the coop and covered it with a polythene sack. The little quails retired in a huddle in the coop and kept warm. In the mornings they came out and fed voraciously. I gave them more maggots which I obtained from a firm selling bait for fishing. I also gave them as much protein as I could, feeding them diced suet or fat along with cheese and raw meat. The fat would help to conserve their energy. The protein would keep their flesh firm. I could have gone back to the scientifically balanced diet of turkey crumbs which also included an antibiotic, I believe, but I hesitated to encourage the birds in an unnatural direction. They didn't seem a whit the worse for living as they were living, despite the fact that the light diminished when the greenhouse was snow-covered for several days on end. The frost didn't reach them. I was anxious about that as most ground birds are sensitive to frost and, if they can, will move from any ground that is likely to be chilled by frost.

Once or twice in the course of winter I had to thaw the water dishes. In the meantime the little quails got to know me and no longer fluttered or ran away when I approached. One began to feed from my fingers and lost all fear of me completely. I was excited about this, especially when this little character would hop over my fingers to eat standing on my palm. The nature of all birds and animals varies. There are characters among birds just as there are characters among men. One will show no fear and behave with trust while the rest reveal their inhibition and instinctively retreat from a hand that offers the most tempting morsel of food. Why this should be I have never been able to discover. My son once had a buzzard that loved to ride on the carrier of a butcher's delivery bicycle which the boy borrowed and rode home upon from time to time, and an aunt had a pet hen that would come right into the farm kitchen, fly up onto her outstretched arm, settle upon her hand and there, after a minute or two of concentration, deposit her egg. My quail didn't quite achieve this unusual rapport but when they began to pipe and display that spring I knew that they would soon begin to lay. They were sheltered. The spring sunshine was filtered to them by the glass of the greenhouse and their enclosure. I boiled some eggs and gave them both the hard yolk and the white as well as some crumbs of sweet biscuit. They suddenly began to lay. It happened in May, a little earlier than the partridge or the pheasant in the wild. I collected first one or two eggs and then half a dozen. I kept them carefully and turned and moistened them so that they remained fit for incubation under one of the birds should any of them become broody. It seemed to me that they were reverting to the natural cycle of laying and there was no reason to suppose that when their body temperature rose they shouldn't brood their own youngsters.

The progress the quail had made encouraged me. I had, after all, brought them back from a controlled room temperature, enabled them to scratch and feed naturally. They had started to lay, stimulated not by artificial means but by the daily improvement in the light and the gentle warmth of the sun. When not one of the hens showed the slightest inclination to nest or lay two eggs in one place, for that matter, I began to see that I was going to have to be lucky to get my quail going. Regretfully I made an omelette of the first gathering of eggs. I ate quite a few more but all of this was to give me time to set about designing and making my own small temperature-controlled incubator, using an immersion-heater rod, a switch and what is known as a pig-lamp. The eggs had to be kept at around 98 degrees. The switch had to operate within five degrees if everything was to go perfectly and I had to check that this didn't mean five degrees below the critical warmth or five above, either of which might spoil the batch. I used a maximum-minimum indicating thermometer to check the overnight switch on and switch off of the heater bulb. When this was all working properly I constructed a tray to hold the marble-like eggs of the birds, each not much larger than the egg of a thrush or blackbird. All that remained was to gather a batch of eggs and set the whole thing up within ten days of beginning to collect the batch, for stale eggs produce a high percentage of failure. I had other things to contend with: the infertility of some eggs due to the continual inbreeding of my stock and the weakness of the bumblebee sized chicks that would hatch if all went well.

When the time came to set up my home-made incubator and brooder I was nervous about leaving the batch of eggs and stayed to see the lamp switch off and come on again. This happened inside an hour. I prayed that it would continue to happen throughout the period of twenty to twenty-three days during which the embryo would germinate and develop. I went in each morning, turned each egg, shielding the incubator from all draught and making sure that my hands were warm. I dampened the shells with lukewarm water and noted the date and temperature. I wasn't doing anything that the scientists or the lab assistant wasn't doing with professional equipment and better technique but I felt sure that if I hatched my own birds from those I had acclimatised they would eventually come to incubate their own eggs. I had, after all, been conditioning my quail to a different environment. They were several degrees more natural than any in the laboratory battery. I began to gain confidence. After ten days I was sure that I would have a hatch of perhaps twenty or thirty quail chicks. I had reckoned without a disaster outside the whole business of making an incubator. On the nineteenth day or the twentieth night there was a power cut. I came down that morning and thought nothing about the electricity supply, for the power had failed around midnight and come on again in the morning. Our chiming grandfather clock reminded me that it was time to go and check my eggs. We were coming to the critical moment. Tomorrow, the day after or the day after that, the first little beak would chip the first shell and soon I would have handfuls of little balls of fluff, a fraction of the size of even a bantam chick newly emerged from the egg!

My thermometer showed that in the night the minimum had fallen. I couldn't believe it. The eggs were much too cool to my touch. At that moment the second power cut happened. The pig-lamp blinked and went out and I knew that it hadn't reacted to the bar of the improvised thermostat cooling down. I laid a woollen cloth over the eggs and went away. The power remained off for two or three hours during which I could have brought the eggs indoors and maintained their warmth somehow but I waited, thinking the power would return at any minute. When it finally did come on I sighed with relief. Two days later the first chick hatched. There was another power cut almost at once. I 'brooded' the only quail I was to see break the shell. All the others died, five or six eggs proved infertile and my solitary chick wasn't a strong specimen. It died in a day. I knew then that I should have set everything up with one of the old-fashioned oil incubators that convert into brooders. I should have candled my eggs and rejected the useless ones.

That summer I went on a game conservancy course and talked to the experts about my plans to establish the Japanese quail. They had their own plans for the Japanese pheasant, a green pheasant, as hardy as a mountain goat. It came from the northern island of Japan and everything about it encouraged the transplanting of the green pheasant from Japan to the northern areas of

Britain which are notoriously less hospitable to the common or garden British gamebird. The quail, however, was a very different proposition, I was told. Like all quails it dislikes the frost. It moves as the ground cools and the small insects die and the small seeds are garnered and gleaned by the great variety of seed-eating birds that haunt stubbles and grass fields after harvest. The quails would manage well until they detected the onset of frosts and then they would slip away, as hard to detect as the landrail or the waterrail. They would move south, on and on, down across the Channel and south into Spain and Italy. They would never come quite so far north again, perhaps. Even the European quail had declined in numbers in its ancient haunts. It was as rare as the corncrake in most places. My little quail would never populate my private jungle!

I found it hard to accept this. My quail had survived a very hard winter. They were hardier birds than when they had first come to me and I saw them taking up quarters in sheltered places, like the weather-wise partridge. The fact that they didn't belong didn't seem a major drawback. The French partridge doesn't belong to Britain and yet it seems to be the bird to replace our own little brown bird of the furrows, the English partridge that threatens to reach the point of no return according to some people, every five or six years. Keeping my Japanese quail on into a second spring was more than a sentimental gesture, although I had become fonder of them every day. I hoped that in the second spring one or two would nest in the orthodox fashion and brood a clutch of eggs. Alas, this didn't happen. In the spring, glossy with the bright sheen of condition on their plumage, the little cocks set up to fight one another again. There was much piping and displaying. Eggs were laid indiscriminately and ignored. This time I ate the eggs. I hadn't the time to spare to begin on an incubation experiment as I might have done had I had a broody bantam hen. A bantam hen could have brought off a clutch of quail eggs without fear of power cuts and there would have been no need to watch the thermometer or concern myself whether a chick fed on the critical day when its 'internal' nourishment was exhausted.

What was I to do with this small colony of quails? I couldn't return them to the people who had given them to me. I couldn't eat them. It would be futile to let them loose without a gradual introduction to the perils of the open field—the sort of thing a keeper has to do when he rears and releases pheasant pullets. Even if they were set free and managed to survive they would have a hazardous journey from Wales to the southern part of Europe. I put off the decision and went on feeding them maggots, ants and insects of other kinds. It looked as though I had a problem similar to that of my sheep-keeping days.

There used to be quail on the island of Anglesey. Maybe a few wander north and breed there yet for the corncrake is heard once in a while in this part of the world although it is rarely if ever seen. I felt that the best place for my brood was the flat country of Anglesey where until a few years ago the fox was unknown and the only danger might be from the hawk or the falcon. I talked to a friend about this and he made some enquiries of a man who was interested in birds of all kinds and would look after the quails, promising to be careful that they weren't exposed to the hunting cat or some playful puppy dog before they learned about the hard world in which they might ultimately fly free. I hesitated for a few days and then went into the long greenhouse, reached into the pen and caught each of my birds very gently and put it in a travelling box. The last to come to my hand was the tame one. Somehow it seemed to sense that things were about to change and I was parting with them.

Some time elapsed before I was able to enquire about the quails. The reply I got made me a little anxious for their welfare but I couldn't complain. I had, after all, given

them away and their fate was no longer in my hands.
I asked again a little later and the information I received
convinced me that they had either been let loose or, much
more likely, ended up on a roasting tin, providing a meal
for someone who had always wanted to know how it felt
to dine like a gourmet!

I suppose I went the wrong way about the whole
business. A scientist would have enquired into the life
and background of the Japanese quail. A student of
animal behaviour and the reaction of birds to a radical
change in their environment would have shaken his head
and said keep the poor creatures in the miserable world
that they have been bred for, the cage, the ounce or two
of turkey crumbs and the tepid water drip. A dreamer
would have enjoyed my dream of diminutive Japanese
quails rising from every pasture, hay or cornfield, and
whirring over the nearest hedge. A sentimental dreamer
would have listened enraptured to the piping of the little
fighting cocks in the breeding season and the world
would have been a better place, populated by quails as a
result of my dreams, but all of this was not to be. I was a
misguided fellow. The experts told me so. I sighed and
thought about the way I had shown those bright-eyed
miniature partridges the way of a beetle on a mountain of
earth, the laborious carrying to and fro of shovelled-up
ants transporting their pupae from one place to another,
and the endless looping of a caterpillar climbing a tall
branch.

One should never do anything of this kind without
responsibility, without some sense of the implications of
putting down a new species in a strange land. Too many
people have helped nature along and given us all kinds
of problems, the problem of how to contain the rabbit
which never was a native in Britain but a warrener
established in colonies, the grey squirrel, the ring dove,
the fat-tailed dormouse, even a wallaby or two in the
Derbyshire Peak District. All of these have come and

plagued us, to say nothing of fur-bearing creatures that didn't live up to expectation—the mink and the musk rat. I must admit that I can see no harm in the quail, would it only stay and share the world with me. One day I may try again for now I have broody bantams and a little experience behind me. If the quail did go south before the frost, might it not establish a migratory pattern like other summering birds and come back to the place of its birth once a year?

7

Bees in my Bonnet

A GREAT many beekeepers suffer from a delusion that they have a very special understanding of bees and an almost mystical way with them that accounts for success. I hold another opinion and that is that bees react to gentle handling. They are stimulated to respond and attack anyone who comes near them making noise or creating vibration and a minor earthquake in the colony. It is as simple as that. Disturb a colony once, and go back again while they are still not settled down, and you are facing the equivalent of an angry bear! I once walked into the angry bear. I was afraid of bees from that day on. I was a small boy then. My grandfather was my idol. He kept bees and worked with them with the minimum of protection for himself. He always had a calmness which he often displayed before an angry bull or a restive horse. It was something a child could see. There was a day when Grandfather went to get his heather honey and walked off with crate after crate of it, puffing his pipe and wearing a face veil that was no more than a bit of fine lace draped over his hat. I went to see what else there might be in the honey-scented beeboxes. The bees fell upon me and sent me screaming away, stumbling over the boulders in that corner of the field, getting up again and feeling the stab of bee-sting after bee-sting on my soft cheeks, around my eyes, my mouth and every other exposed part of my body. The following day I still couldn't see the light, my face was so swollen. I knew then that a bee colony isn't a collection of bees but a huge animal in itself, a monster quite capable of making man take to his heels, bringing him down and taking his life, perhaps, with an enormous injection of poison.

It was all very well to go swarm-chasing. Swarming bees are docile, drunk on honey and not at all aggressive unless their queen is threatened. We all went swarm-chasing when the occasion arose. We had to. Grandfather insisted upon it. But the whole business, even a long treasured memory of helping to get a wild colony out of a dead tree, left me with a feeling that I would never keep bees. Bees are not to be petted and not to be won over. They have no fear to begin with. They neither trust nor love man. He is a scent, a shadow, a giant looming over their world, and they will die to drive him off. I told myself I would never be a beekeeper.

Never is not a long time. It is outside time altogether. The word is one used with indifference to its true meaning, without conception of eternity or infinity! I smile now at the way things turned out. My grandfather was a bee-keeper. My father kept bees. I, in turn, keep them and see myself doing so as long as I have the strength to lift a super of honey or turn the handle of a separator. Things happen sometimes to make me wonder if a man can escape his destiny and avoid what is in the blood! There was a time when I never took scone or pancake without it overspilling the honey layered upon it, when I never had a cough without it being eased for me—in the middle of the night more often than not—by my nose being held to make my mouth open and the overflowing dessert or tablespoonful of heather honey being tipped down my throat.

Honey has mystical properties for some people. It is like the business of vintage wine. Its blend will never be exactly repeated in another year, and certainly not in another place, because of the flowers and blossom of trees that happen to flourish and appear at particular times. The connoisseur of wines knows what lies behind the vintage. He knows the amount of sunshine, the elements of the soil, the humidity or the dryness of a season, the sum of days between fruit and ferment, and a thousand other things that make a very special brew. The man who eats honey is hardly aware of the parallel. He knows only sweetness and a delicate colour or flavour. He rarely appreciates that honey is even more extraordinary than the product of the vineyard. I knew nothing of this, and thought less about it when I was a boy.

My grandfather died. His bees died. There is a plausible tale about this kind of happening. One should tell the bees that there has been a death, they say. The bees, however, are, as I have said, a wild bear, a sleeping monster. They neither love nor hate. Death comes to most of them in six or seven weeks. They know nothing of death, either. They live to work and death is at the end. No one told my grandfather's bees that he was dead. We were all concerned with our emotions. His bees died for the very simple reason that no one looked in at them at all to see whether they needed candy, syrup or perhaps some honey to tide them through from the cold, hard days of early spring, until the clover bloomed and the roadside was studded with purple-bloomed hard-heads, attractive to the bumblebee.

'Grandfather's bees died,' I was told. I remember looking at the derelict row of hives with nettles and thorns growing up around them and hens working their way into their shelter to lay-away. It made me sad to think how the old man would plod to and from that corner and gently pick off bees that entangled themselves in the hairs of his beard, releasing them so that they could fly back to the hive. There was something of him there yet. His had been the last hand to raise or lower the lids of the hives. He alone could say exactly what lay within. All we knew was that no bees came and went. The hives were like the old moorland cothouses, unoccupied, sleeping in the sun, wearing, weathering and mouldering away. No one kept bees there after that. In a while the wooden hives rotted and were completely lost in the brambles and thorns that took over the corner. The structures lost shape, sagged and went down like some old, long-disused garden privy, the last remnants of wood turning moss-green like the trunk of a tree growing in some shaded, dank corner.

My father had never understudied his father in the business. Beekeeping isn't a hobby in the eyes of the uninitiated but rather a kind of eccentricity, a quirk in a man's nature that makes him meddle with a colony of winged insects. That this is so was brought home to me not so long ago by an acquaintance, who knew nothing about the honey bee, asking me how I got them all in one box and having got them there, kept them together, all working for me. Everyone has some belief, either in God, a great design, a pattern of evolution. Man happens to have discovered how to exploit the colony bee that stores honey. Why the honey bee stores honey is quite simple. It must live through the year when there is no source of material for its manufacture, but who can say why a dandelion blooms in the spring and charlock in early summer and heather in August or, if they can explain as much, why at those times and without fail?

My own ultimate venture into beekeeping would have seemed less accidental had I thought about my father. He began to keep bees when his father had been dead for perhaps ten years. He established his colonies in his garden in Cheshire and immediately began to harvest more honey than he knew what to do with. He made mead although he was a comparatively temperate man and for the greater part of his life had known neither the taste of strong drink nor the flavour of tobacco. I suppose he

drank his mead. He certainly never offered me any when
I went home. Once he was stung so badly that he was
violently sick, but he persisted in saying that his bees
never stung him. It was a matter of pride with him. The
truth was that he had been stung so often that he no
longer felt the stings and most of the time was so well-
immunised that the poison had no effect upon his system.
I admitted my nervousness of bees. I couldn't conceal it,
but one evening when I lived in an overgrown village
on the Welsh coast I was about to enter my garden when
I discovered a swarm of bees hanging in a tree right at my
gate. A kind of madness got into me. I would take the
swarm, box it, and put it on the railway to my father!
My experience of swarm-taking was limited to the chase.
I had been a banger of pot-lids, a manufacturer of the
artificial storm that was at one time thought to make
swarming bees come back to earth, settle and allow themselves to be taken. I nevertheless determined to do as I
had planned. I got myself a wooden box with a sliding lid,
a box big enough to accommodate thirty thousand bees,
or a prime swarm. I drilled small holes in the lid so that
the bees, once enclosed, could breathe. I prepared a
fastener for the box and a label and went in search of a
ladder and climbed the tree with the box in my arms
and a pair of secateurs in one hand. With what I was
consciously aware was bravery, I gently cut the branch
and stood firm when the loaded tip dropped into the box.
A few bees milled round my head. I went gently back
down the ladder, slid the lid of the box in place and firmly
fixed the fastener. The box was labelled 'Perishable. Bees.
Do not shake! Urgent! Delivery at earliest!' I got in my
car, drove to the station and handed the box over. It went
off on the first train. No one along the way wanted to
keep such humming, angry creatures a moment longer
than necessary. Two hours later my father telephoned to
congratulate me. The swarm, a big one, had just been
collected at the station. The parcels department had

telephoned him to come and take the thing away at once. I went to bed feeling very satisfied with myself. I never bothered to ask my father how those native Welsh bees fared inland in a different climate. I didn't really know enough about bees to know that they might not take to a different sort of country.

My next experience was wished upon me. In a village people talk. My taking of the swarm had earned me a certain reputation as a man used to handling bees. No one in his right mind would have done what I had done unless he had the know-how! My next door neighbour but one was a Welsh Baptist minister and a friend. It was the custom in his chapel to invite a minister from another district to give the sermon on certain occasions and when this happened the visiting minister would be accompanied by his wife and receive hospitality and bed and board in the house of the minister whose chapel he was visiting. Welsh Baptists, like many other Welsh non-conformist churches and chapels, have a service in the morning and Sunday school in the afternoon. Sunday school is not simply a place where children are taught the scriptures but a religious gathering attended by the faithful members of the chapel aged from five to ninety-five. It was just after Sunday school that our doorbell rang and there stood my friend and neighbour looking very concerned. The best bedroom of his house, prepared for his guests, was full of bees. His second best bedroom was being invaded and it seemed that the whole upstairs would soon be full of flying bees. Could I please help? I was, after all, a man who could persuade bees to go into a box and move them out of the county. I had some special power. I had demonstrated that!

I said nothing in reply to these compliments. I could only have reproached the good Christian minister with a certain lapse into pagan belief. I smiled and said I was not an expert but I would come and look at the invaders. They were like a plague in Egypt, said my friend, a scourge! He had opened the windows and, would I believe him, more bees had come in and none that he could see had gone out! I walked with a brave look on my face, conscious of the fact that we were being watched, as one is always being watched in a village. What was wrong at the minister's house? they asked each other as they peeped from behind their curtains. They were used to the minister being sent for and the reason for his being summoned was easily guessed, but what did the minister need with me, an incomer, a foreigner and not even a Baptist! I went into the minister's house aware of the humming of bees. One or two went in with me. There was a smell of honey in the house.

'I think you have had these bees for a long time,' I said.

The minister said it was possible but they had never shown themselves before. Why should they suddenly come out from the cracks in his floorboards, creep from under the skirtings and set up a humming that made it hard to ignore them? I thought back to my childhood. The bees were swarming. They were looking for a place for the new queen within the same house, in a cavity under the same floor, perhaps. I could see how they normally went in and out through a ventilator brick between the ceiling of the downstairs room and the bedroom above. Now, it seemed to me, the bees were moving. A new queen had emerged. The old queen was departing. The new queen and her drones would soon take a nuptial flight. The whole business, if it continued under one roof, would go on for days. The property would become a vast beehive, given time! I said this as a joke. My friend was alarmed and I hastened to promise that I would clear his house of bees or die in the attempt! I would stay with it, even if he and his fellow minister had to sit downstairs consoling their wives until dawn. I wondered if I had lost my reason. I really hadn't much idea how I could perform the miracle. It wasn't a thing for the bell, book and candle. In any case, that was more in the clergyman's line.

Upstairs in the bedroom, where the curtains were drawn against the late summer afternoon sun, I could barely see across the bed for bees. I went hesitantly to the corner of the room where they seemed to be emerging faster than anywhere else and managed to prise up a floorboard. Ten thousand more bees arose and flew round my head, but they stung me not. I thought about the prayer book and the terror, and a thousand falling at my right hand. I had some slight acquaintance with the Anglican Church although I was baptised a Presbyterian! I closed the windows and replaced the floorboard while I went off and improvised a smoker from a cocoa tin lashed to a pair of bellows. I managed to make my eyes water and almost choked myself puffing smoke through cracks in the floor. The device certainly worked. More and more bees came up from the floor and sailed round the room. Where there had been a hundred we had a thousand, where we had had a thousand perhaps twenty thousand! Who could count bees in a darkened bedroom? I had another inspiration. I had a spray which I could charge with DDT (let good beekeepers shudder and hold up their hands in horror!). The spray did what the smoke had done. It brought out more bees. The minister retreated to take tea and convoy his guests to the chapel for the evening service. I brooded and wondered how I could possibly save my face, let alone secure the bedroom for the good Christians who hoped to occupy it with nothing to disturb them but cockcrow in the morning.

I was still brooding when the ministers and their wives came back from chapel at the slow pace of chapel-goers devoutly considering the sermon. Like the people of the village street, I peeped from behind the curtain and wondered what they were saying.

'I am sure my friend will have found a way of getting rid of the bees,' my neighbour was saying.

'I am sure.'

But the bees were already out on the landing and night was at hand. The light was fading. Where would they settle except on the floor, on the beds, on the lavatory seat perhaps? There were a few in the bath! Inspiration is a thing that has come to me more than once in my life. I switched on the light in the bedroom and the bees rushed towards it like moths. They came from the landing, from the unlit rooms, the shadows of the bathroom, the floor. I watched them and knew in that moment I had them all in one room, give or take two or three. I could shut the door. If I turned off the light the bees would be in almost complete darkness. I switched it off and waited a moment or two. It seemed to me that quite a few settled not on the floor but on the counterpane and the pillows of the bed. I switched the light off after I had dragged off the blankets and exposed the bedsheet. A minute or so later I put it on again and the sheet was almost black with swarming bees. Now I had them! Now I knew how to perform the miracle. I went downstairs to meet the men of the cloth.

'Have a cup of tea,' I said. 'The bees are still there but I have the answer. In an hour, God willing, they will be gone!'

I am afraid the use of God's name didn't exactly bring a smile to the faces of either of them and when I asked for the Hoover cleaner I could see that they thought I had gone mad. The cleaner was produced by the minister's wife.

'I hope you can do what you promise,' she said with a gentle smile. 'We couldn't sleep in a bed with bees.'

'I will put the bees to bed first and then remove them,' I said. The electric socket for the cleaner was on the landing. I plugged the thing in and went to the bedroom, switched on the light, and lifted the cleaner onto the bed, keeping it running nicely all the while. In a minute I had 'hoovered up' all the bees that remained long enough to be sucked in by the fan. Out with the light, a pause, on with the light when all the bees were settled on the bed. The Hoover hummed and the clean-up was repeated. I was winning! I hurried down and emptied the cleaner bag and hurried back again.

'What are you doing up there?' they asked.

'Hoovering,' I said.

The dustbin held ten thousand corpses. The cleaner bag had been packed tight with them. It filled again. I don't know how long it took but at last it was time for me to go. I opened the window and let the smoky smell waft away. I gathered up my tools and went down to the living room.

'Not a bee to be seen,' I announced. 'They have all gone. I will empty the Hoover and go home.'

I had to have a cup of tea, of course, but at last I went home. In the gloom at the corner of the wall I could see a few bees forlornly flying round the ventilation brick entrance to their 'hive'. They were the remnants of the colony. I had overcome them without the jawbone of an ass, but for a little while it had seemed that the minister would have to evacuate his house. No one was stung. I had enhanced a reputation for being a master of bees but I doubt whether any self-respecting beekeeper would have spoken to me after hearing what I had done to that swarming colony in the minister's house.

My apparent fearless handling of the bees encouraged the minister. It is a strange thing that certain professions seem attracted to beekeeping. Clerics and doctors, for instance, are often caught up in the hobby. The one, I suppose, because he wonders at the wisdom of the Creator and the other because he is of a scientific mind. Before I knew what he had done my neighbour had set up his first beehive on the garden slope. His bees propagated my apple trees. I could see them winging their way across the hill on a summer's day, but then one or two of these winging bees collided with the wife of a member of his congregation. Terrified of being stung, the lady clutched at her hair, staggered, struck out at the bees, and fell backwards down some concrete steps. This was a disaster. The minister felt he had to move his bees rather than let them be a nuisance to his neighbours. He moved them to a farm up the road and more by luck than anything else, for the farm was within the radius of the colony's normal foraging from the garden, the moving proved successful. Here, however, there was another drawback. The farmer had a young family and they roamed about and were fatally curious about bees. The minister was compelled to give up.

While this had been going on, my father had retired and come to live in the house which, since his death, has been my home. He had brought with him all his bee colonies, moving them on repeated journeys from north Cheshire to North Wales and only once having a little trouble when the bees in a hive on the back seat of the car decided to leak out and he had to pull up and abandon ship in the middle of the traffic through the city of Chester. The bees were persuaded to go back into the hive by a simple expedient. The car was obscured from daylight by some old army blankets carried in the boot. The bees retired to the hive. The hive was effectively sealed and father drove on to establish a dozen or more colonies on the Welsh coast. The minister had heard about my Father's apiary. Could his troublesome colony be absorbed into it? Father readily agreed and we transported the minister's bees without trouble. They were, however, an upset colony. From the disturbances they had suffered in a single season they acquired an aggressiveness that made them almost impossible to handle. The minister came and looked at them once and shook his head sadly. He decided they were a bad lot. They were, in fact, what man had made them.

My father's beekeeping in Wales was far less successful than it had been in Cheshire. He never took honey from any of his colonies. Year after year the bees just held their own and Father was resigned to getting no harvest. My mother died and he lost interest in bees and beekeeping. He had, after all, so many other things to do that required everyday attention and he couldn't manage it all. He was taken ill within the year and died eighteen months after Mother. The bee colonies faded away. I came to live at the cottage and looked at the long row of well-painted, soundly-made hives (he had built them himself and they had many refinements). What use were they to me? Occasionally, I noticed, bees would come and scout these old hives, attracted by the smell of beeswax and propolis, which is a resinous substance with which bees seal and fasten together all loose parts of a beehive. I vaguely wondered if the hives would be occupied by swarms. I had no intention of setting up as a beekeeper, and when I went on holiday one summer I met a man whose enthusiasm for bees and beekeeping was boundless. Who would appreciate the offer of fourteen beehives more than a man who already had beehives all round him and hoped to expand his apiary? A truck was sent up to the cottage and all the beehives loaded on it. I had things to do, clearing up old hen-runs, mending old glasshouses.

Ten years passed. A friend in the town down below had a neighbour who was a minister and kept bees, not in his back garden but 'farmed out' in the countryside, one or two here, and one or two there where farmers gave permission. The friend sent the minister to me. Would I have any objection to his keeping a few colonies of bees on my land? I said I didn't mind at all. We had enough room. I knew something about bees for my grandfather had kept them and my father too, although I wanted nothing to do with them myself! The minister brought his bees. In due course of time he gave me a jar of honey. We talked about bees more and more. 'I think,' he said, one day, 'I will make you a beekeeper.' I suppose it was easier evangelism than bringing me back to the Church. I shook my head and said no. I had watched the whole business. It was not for a man of my temperament. Used to managing his elders, the minister wouldn't take no for an answer. He rang me up one day and said, 'I have a present for you. A beehive and a newly-taken prime swarm of bees. I will set them up for you, feed them, bring them through the winter and next spring you will take them over!'

He was such a kind fellow that I couldn't refuse. I went down to help put the finishing touches to the carpentry of a renovated hive. Wearing a veil, some gloves and wellington boots to keep the bees from climbing my trouser legs, I went off to bring the swarm home. The hive stood in the corner of the orchard. Just before dusk we tipped the colony onto a sheet and watched them slowly march into their new premises. They had some syrup and a little honey waiting for them. I knew then that I had caught the fever. I was going to be a beekeeper in spite of everything I had said.

The colony was established in late May. There is an old rhyme about the value of bee swarms. A swarm of bees in May is worth a load of hay, a swarm in June a silver spoon, but a swarm in July hardly worth a fly. My colony did well. The minister came and together we took the honey they had so quickly gathered, leaving enough for them to get through the winter. It wasn't a lot of honey, fifteen or sixteen pounds, but how sweet it was, how clear and golden. I had never tasted anything like it! I began to work out how much honey I would get next season as eagerly as a gambler works out the odds and dreams himself into making a fortune. I began almost at once on the building of a second beehive, ruefully thinking of the wonderful hives my father had built. I would build all my own hives. I would buy another stock of bees and take swarms. Soon I would have a large apiary, as many bees as my father had and more!

There are two popular types of beehive. One is known as a National and consists of a series of crates that sit neatly on top of one another, the deeper bottom crate holding the brood frame and housing the queen and her retinue, and the smaller crates above, separated from the brood crate by what is known as a queen excluder, serving as a storehouse for the honey gathered by the workers. This type of hive isn't as warm as what is known as the W.B.C., a hive designed by a gentleman by the name of W. B. Carr. The W.B.C. hive incorporates more timber and is more difficult for the do-it-yourself carpenter to construct, but I remembered my father had favoured the W.B.C. which, by virtue of its outer shell and separate crates within, gives better insulation from the cold and is much more weatherproof. It took me a week or two to build my first hive and fit it out. Before the winter was over I had built a second, learning a little from my previous mistakes. Now, I told myself as spring approached, I would soon have three colonies of bees and be facing the problem of how to house the fourth.

My bees wintered well. I was advised to wait a little while and buy a stock of bees from a reliable supplier. One thing I hadn't realised was that my bees were subject to inspection by the Ministry of Agriculture and Fisheries in the form of an official known as the Foul Brood Inspector. I had never heard of this before, but sure enough the Foul Brood man arrived at my door.

8

Honey Harvests

MY wife would hardly believe that such an official could exist. A Foul Brood Inspector! She had heard of sanitary inspectors and a host of other men whose official titles belied the unpleasantness of their trades or professions. The giver-out of official titles had been unkind to this poor fellow. That was plain. If his title was a reliable indication of the art he practised, then obviously he had an unpleasant task to perform, but what was foul brood? Was it something a person could have without being aware of it, like B.O.? Hiding her amusement, she welcomed the Inspector. He could search where he liked. She was pretty certain he wouldn't find anything foul. The Inspector bedecked himself in his regalia and went off to open my beehive. I learned afterwards that he really didn't need to open a hive to tell whether it was suffering from American Foul Brood or not, for its odour is enough. The disease, highly contagious to bees, could very quickly spread throughout the country. It could spell disaster for much more than the bee-stocks or the beekeepers. With the main pollinators of blossom and flowers killed off we might starve for want of clover, fruit, new seed for another season. Birds and animals in turn would be affected. The pattern of ecology is elaborate. The Americans didn't invent the disease but it seems to have emanated from the other side of the Atlantic, and although there is a native strain of foul brood, it is said to be not nearly so dangerous. The Ministry very rightly employs a man who knows a little more than the average person about beekeeping and the diseases to which bees are subject. When foul brood is discovered there is only one remedy. Like the advent of foot and mouth, slaughter must follow. Bee colonies found to be infected are destroyed. The combs are burned and the hive is never used again. It, too, may be burned.

The Inspector found no foul brood, of course, but he did mention in passing that he had been told I wanted another stock of bees. Through his connections in the business he could obtain a reliable stock for me. I could also have the hive the bees were in and he would transport the whole thing to me. The price would be no more than eight pounds. I was delighted when the new stock arrived. I now had two occupied hives and two hives awaiting swarms. I should have waited but I couldn't wait. Off I went to buy a four frame nucleus, that is, a queen and four frames containing a certain amount of sealed and unsealed brood, some honey stock to go with the brood, and as many bees as had been established in the mini-hive known as a nuclei box. I brought the nucleus back and set them up in one of my newly-made hives. They were what are known as Israeli bees, a Near-East strain of bee, known to be docile and manageable. I thought how hard the Israeli people work and hoped that the Palestinian bees would prove as industrious. To help the nucleus along I decided to add brood frames from my other two colonies. This is something not infrequently done by beekeepers who want to take a short-cut. A novice may do it, but he must think about it carefully. I did my thinking rather quickly and could hardly wait to carry the plan out. It meant opening the hive containing the nucleus and the adjoining hive from which I would steal a frame of brood. Since I needed two frames of brood to build the stock I would open my other hive as well and steal from it too. Get it all over at once, I told myself. Do it all on the same morning, quickly, neatly and with the minimum of disturbance.

I dressed for the part and lit my smoker with which I would repel or control the three colonies while I manipulated them. No one ever marched into battle more confidently! No one knowing anything about bees could have picked a worse time for I went soon after nine in the morning. At noon most of the more virile and aggressive bees, the foragers, are abroad on missions, bringing back honey, nectar, pollen. In the morning they may be still lingering over breakfast, and mine were. To make matters worse, I was half way into the work when my smoker gave up and I had to make up my mind to continue without it. I decided that I must. Just then I began to see bees before my eyes. They were inside my veil. It seemed to me in that moment of panic that there were more bees inside the veil than out! I had changed the hat that carried the veil because I had found the brim cracked. Bees might have penetrated through that crack. Instead of the old Panama hat I had clapped my fishing hat on my head and brought the veil down over that, forgetting that a fishing hat has no continuous brim. In fact it has a peak fore and aft. The bees, clustering on my hat simply poured down past my ears and busily set about trying to sting me to death!

I knew the agony of so many stings that I simply had to back off. The bees came with me. They came from each of the three colonies I had opened and followed me every yard of the way. I began to be afraid. I didn't know where to go. I started up the path towards the wood and they swarmed on me. My arms were black with bees, or black and brown, for the Israeli bees are sandy coloured. I discovered that the attackers intended to follow me wherever I went. I turned and headed for the potting shed where I had a spare hat, another veil. They came with me and stung me even in the darkness of the shed. I stripped to the skin regardless of being stung again and again and quickly dressed in an old shirt I kept there, another jacket, the new veil and old felt hat that hung behind the door. I stood for a minute and decided I had to go through with it, no matter what happened. I must close the three hives and withdraw, but only after I had done what I had set out to do. I must act quickly or there would be some risk of the three colonies being chilled.

It took all the courage I could summon to walk back to the hives and return to the fray. I carefully put the new frames in the small colony, straightened everything up and closed it down. I then tackled the larger and much angrier colonies on either side. When I had finished I plodded back to the shed and took off my regalia. The smoker was like an amateur's pipe, too tightly packed to stay alight. I cursed myself for not having taken the precaution of seeing that it was burning well before setting out to the hives. I also made a mental note of something I had read about novices being lulled into a false sense of security by going to their bees before mid-day and finding they were rarely attacked or only stung once or twice. I hadn't thought about that. Now I knew. I had forty stings on my neck, chest and face. There may have been more. I counted forty because I could see and scrape off forty. I tidied myself up and walked into the kitchen and said, 'I've been stung.' I wasn't understating the position. I couldn't think of any other way of putting it. Badly stung? How many stings before a man is badly stung? How many before he dies? I didn't really know. I only knew that I had had as many bee-stings as I could take, and I wasn't going to die. In a strange way I felt elated, not about the fact that I had survived. The stings had produced a strange lifting of my spirits and a feeling of well-being which I had experienced on occasions when I had donated blood. The total physical effect of so many stings didn't come for an hour or two. I had some business

to do and drove the car. I was away about an hour. On the
return journey I found that I couldn't see so much of the
horizon. I could see the road through the slits of swollen
eyelids, swollen brows and cheeks. My chin and neck
were fast becoming as even as the trunk of a tree. I put
the car away and came indoors and went and laid down
on the bed. There was considerable pain from the swelling
but I was not unhappy. I had no need of a doctor. I didn't
want to eat for the time being. My eating muscles were
slightly distended, to say the least!

For two days I looked like the loser of a world heavy-
weight championship fight. People smiled at me, even
grinned and expressed their sympathy. 'Bees?' they said.
'Wouldn't go near them! You can die of bee-stings. You
know that?' Oddly enough, that morning on the radio
there had been news of an unfortunate lady who had been
attacked by bees while her son-in-law was working with
one of his colonies. The lady had died. Well, I said, I had
had some fear of being killed by so many bees, but only
for a moment. Bees probably only killed people whose
hearts weren't sound.

The Foul Brood Inspector made a second, unofficial
visit and talked to my wife. He had a story about bee-
stings that changed my outlook. It seemed that in his
early days he had been in the habit of examining bee
colonies without gloves, veil or any sort of protection.
He had suffered his quota of painful stings and had
become 'immunised'. Thereafter he never bothered to
count how many stings he took or how often he was stung
by each colony. Perhaps he had three hundred stings in a
matter of days. It may have been more. It could have
been less, but he was certainly stung a great many times
in a season. One day he went to inspect a colony and was
stung. The attack was hardly an attack at all. One or two
stings were all he suffered before his breathing became
inhibited. He gasped and staggered and went down. A
doctor was brought and the unfortunate man was rushed

off to Liverpool, being given oxygen all the way. He had reached the limit. One sting might have been all that was needed to kill him. Thereafter, he said, he had never gone to inspect bees without taking every possible precaution, wearing gloves, wellington boots, a well-tucked-in veil held out from the face by a stiff and broad-brimmed hat.

There was a message for me. It was plain that I was a novice and novices tend to think that the danger doesn't exist, especially when they see bee-handling demonstrated by vain fellows who don't reveal that they have taken frames of young, immature bees away from a large colony at noon. These young bees are docile. The handler in one case I had witnessed, wore an open cricket shirt and khaki shorts! It had all seemed so simple; so much a matter of personal confidence and a cool head. I didn't let my bees get anywhere near me after that. I may not be the coolest beekeeper in the world but I have the greatest respect for the sleeping bear.

Having got so far in the business and taken a little honey, the next test of my way with bees would be to take my seaboard colonies to the moors for heather honey. This is often a second harvest. The heather comes into bloom around grouse-shooting time. Bees placed on the moor at exactly the right time have nothing to do but fly short flights while they fill the combs to bursting point with thick, dark honey. To move a hive one waits until dusk on the eve of the transporting and seals the entrance with a bit of zinc gauze fastened down with a couple of drawing pins. The hives generally moved are the crate-type Nationals. I had W.B.C. hives. These had to be more carefully packed and wrapped. The packing and wrapping was done as darkness fell. At first light in the morning, with the aid of my minister friend, I carried the hives to the little trailer behind the car. It was just big enough to accommodate four National hives or two W.B.C.'s which are much more bulky. This meant two trips to the moor. The minister moved his Nationals after my W.B.C.'s were on the heather. Not a bee escaped. They hummed and buzzed but they couldn't get out. We trundled them away to the moor, a distance of more than twenty miles, and set them up on a fenceline, sheltered from the cold wind. I was relieved when we had accomplished this. People on the way had looked at us with some awe. They weren't used to seeing beehives being towed about, and with so much sacking round them it was evident that the hives weren't empty.

The hives were all set in line before the day was out. There was only one incident that day. Soon after the hives are set down the bees have to be released. On a road journey the temperature of a colony rises as the normal ventilation of the hive tends to be seriously restricted because of the packing and the fact that bees whose menial duty it is to ventilate, or provide the air-conditioning by vibrating their wings at the entrance, are unable to perform this task. As soon as bees are set down on a new site they clamour to be released. They come out full of wrath. We knew all about that. Each hive was opened and a retreat made. We each had more than a halo of bees about our head but we were well-protected. The minister was watching the hives from a distance when I spotted the shepherd coming down the slope. He had his dogs with him and a few sheep. With a wave of his hand he called a greeting in Welsh. The minister turned and responded and proceeded to hurry to the innocent flockmaster to shake his hand. The bees followed. In a minute the shepherd was being stung. His dogs cocked their ears and started back, the sheep scattered. The good minister, still forgetting his retinue of angry bees, attempted to offer assistance by pulling out the stings. The shepherd declined. What he said in Welsh I do not know but I am sure that beneath his veil the minister blushed!

We waited until the few sheep and their master had gone and considered whether we could yet re-enter the

car and divest ourselves of veils and gloves. If we left too
soon the bees that were fixed upon our hats would remain
in the car and make the return journey a little unpleasant.
At last we were able to get into the car and slam the doors
behind us. A few bees were inside, but we carefully put
them out through the window without allowing others
to get in. It didn't take us long to rid ourselves of the
protective clothing and set sail for home. Behind us the
moor was faintly tinged with blue, the blue haze of
evening. The heather bloom wasn't as much in evidence
as we should have liked.

When bees are put on a moor in unfavourable con-
ditions, or when the weather suddenly turns cold or very
wet, the first thing they do, having consumed a good
part of their own reserves, is to rob the colony next door.
Robbing results in starvation. Many beekeepers who have
set out to get heather honey have got none and had to
feed their bees all winter. Another hazard is the bumblebee which will do its best to squeeze its way in through a
restricted opening and feed on whatever honey is to be
found. It is said that it takes three or four honey bees
to eject and kill one bumblebee. When we returned I
counted a pile of thirty-two bumblebees outside one hive!
Had a hundred and twenty honey bees died defending
the stock? I couldn't say. The whole business became
fraught with uncertainty. Instead of the sun shining,
the moorland remained under cloud for five or six days.
A cold wind blew. After that a low mist that was equally
cold stopped the heather buds opening and the bees
from foraging. I counted the days, working out the
probable consumption of stock and the meagre supply
that was being gathered. We were losing fast, I said, after
I had been up to make an inspection. The minister, with
at least twenty years' more experience than I had, agreed.
At the end of ten days the weather changed. The sun
blazed down. We combined a visit to the site with a lazy
afternoon fishing for perch in a small moorland lake. The

perch didn't take very well and no pike moved, but it was all very pleasant. This time when we left we could admire shoulders of purple heather and banks of ling. Even the aftergrowth on the adjoining pasture showed a late clover blossom. It was a reseeded field. Now, surely, the bees couldn't go wrong and we would leave them as long as possible.

It was the weather-wise shepherd who told us when to come and take the hives away. It always got bitterly cold in mid-September on that particular face of the moor, he said. The heather was good. It bloomed later than most places, but it died quickly. We must come and take our bees by mid-September. Once again we had the business of packing and loading hives but the bees in that colder atmosphere were more docile, and more content, for their stores were ample. We got them away with little trouble although the operation took a whole day.

Heather honey is thicker, darker and stronger-flavoured than other kinds. It is also almost impossible to extract from the wax comb by means of a centrifugal extractor. There remain two ways of getting clear heather honey. One is to use a heather honey press which squeezes the honey from the cells and destroys them in the process—the wax can be sold or made into candles! The other is to cut out the centres of the frames, put these in a bag and strain the honey off through muslin. The latter is a slow, sticky process that discourages most beekeepers who live away from the heather from ever putting their bees on it. Having no press, we squeezed the combs and strained the honey through muslin. It was excellent honey. Its distinctive scent and flavour took me back to my childhood, but oh, how hard we had worked to get twenty pounds of the stuff. Who was to say that the late blossom and flowers at home wouldn't have provided just as much honey, and extractable honey at that?

I closed down my hives for the winter. The Israeli bees had stayed at home and, alas, had made next to no progress. I had to feed them. They suffered from a lack of drawn comb. Some strains of bee, I discovered, are poor at drawing out the wax cells which they fill with honey. It is a matter of temperature and there are ways of encouraging bees to draw comb. My foreign bees seemed to be a lazy lot. Come the spring, I said, I would think about finding a new queen for them and killing the old one off, which, in a matter of weeks, changes the nature of the colony completely. I had built two National Hives during the winter and put the Israelis into one of these in the summer, but they were not only poor at drawing comb. They didn't glue the crates together with propolis. A driving south-westerly wind came and rain seeped in. My Israelis didn't survive. I wasn't sorry. I had become a firm believer in local bees, used to the climate.

It wasn't until my third year that I had a prime swarm, or a swarm of any kind. I had by this time discovered how to read signs of imminent swarming. I could even predict the morning and the time, providing the weather was settled. My first swarm took off over the fence at the far end of the old orchard. They settled in the heart of the thickest bramble patch I have ever attempted to penetrate. I was determined to get them, however. It was a point of honour with me not to let my first prime swarm get away. I ploughed into the brambles, getting my legs lacerated in the process, and threw a sack over the clustering bees. In the meantime the weather had become overcast. A fine rain was falling. This was in my favour, if I could work out a way of getting the bees before they were shaken off the individual stalks of bramble and took flight again. I armed myself with some secateurs and began slowly and methodically cutting my way right up to the cluster. I removed the brambles piecemeal, in short sections, often only two or three inches in length. I cleared a wide swath to the swarm and brought up a mini-beehive containing a couple of frames and a small amount of honey. I cut a fresh path round the cluster and advanced upon it from the rear with a properly working smoker. With gentle puffs of smoke I persuaded the whole mass to move over until they were swarming on the little hive. Slowly they began to walk down its front and do as I wanted them to do. I took away the sheltering sack and let the gentle rain encourage them to get a roof over their heads but the whole business took me from eleven o'clock in the morning until ten o'clock at night!

The following day a second swarm came off and went a little farther over, settling on the mouldering timbers of an old peach house, inside which thorns had grown up so thickly that no one could get there. There were brambles all round the outside too. I began again cutting my way to the bees and after an hour or two had them boxed. They too were moved home at nightfall. At least I could take swarms I told myself, but it was soon evident that my second swarm was unhappy. They lingered about the hive. They didn't go out and were aimless. I consulted the books. Somehow the queen had perished, either at the time of swarming or while I was hustling the brown throng into their new quarters. Now I would have to provide the queenless colony with the means of creating a new queen—taking a brood frame with a queen cell attached and placing it in this queenless hive. I did this. In a short time the sealed queen cell I had noticed on the frame I had put in was cut open. A new queen had been born. Nothing happened for three weeks after that but then the colony began to show some purpose in what it was about. Bees went foraging. A small amount of brood was to be seen, new brood, new eggs. The colony had been depleted by a lag between the death of the original queen and the creation of a new one, but with care it came through the winter.

Before the honey harvest that year I gained another prime swarm. This one proved a little more hazardous in the taking. The swarm advertised itself in the morning but rain fell and it didn't emerge. I told myself in the late afternoon that nothing would happen until the following day but I had no sooner eased my mind with this conviction than I heard the bees going. They sailed over the house, a vast armada of bees. I ran out and followed. They moved at a fast walking pace, except that they went over walls and bushes and trees in a straight line. I had to climb and flounder and make detours until I came up with them. They settled in the top of a thirty-five-foot ash tree! Now what was I to do? I stood and thought for a bit. I needed a ladder to get into the lower branches of the tree, a saw and some secateurs perhaps. I would have to gently cut through the long top branch upon which the swarm was now well established and let it slowly lean and creak as it came over to hang near the ground where I could take the bees. I hurried off for the tools and returned to the scene of operations with them and a short ladder. I was ready, but I had overlooked the fact that it is difficult to climb into a tree wearing wellington boots, particularly while it is raining. I remembered this when it was a little too late. I was off the ladder using a saw and gently cutting at the top branch which was almost beyond the length of my arm unless I stretched for all I was worth. I was doing this and had succeeded in getting the branch to begin to topple when my foothold went. It was small wonder that it did. In my enthusiasm I had balanced on my feet alone and put both hands to the saw!

The world turned upside down. I was conscious of my feet being outlined against the sky. I recognised the shape of my wellington boots before I realised that I was falling head-down. My shoulders hit a low branch. My body turned again and I crashed to the ground to end up in a sitting position. I had fallen almost thirty feet into a briar bush! I thought to myself, well, I am alive and no bones broken and began to laugh like a lunatic. The bees began to leave the drooping branch and return to a higher position on another limb of the tree. This time I had had enough. I picked myself up, gathered the tools and the ladder and staggered off home. Let the swarm do what it liked!

My watch was one of those very reliable self-winding ones fastened to my wrist by a link bracelet. I decided, when I found that I wasn't wearing it, that I must have left it in the bathroom, for the first thing I did upon my return home was to have a shower and then a hot bath. I couldn't find the watch anywhere. In the middle of the night I awoke with a pain in my wrist. Along the part of my wrist where the watchband would have been was a red abrasion. I decided that as I had fallen a twig, or some protruding part of the tree, had hooked into the band and ripped the watch from my arm. At six o'clock, when it was light, I got up and went back to the tree. My watch lay on the ground, hidden by the crumpled thorns. It was still going, although it had been raining heavily all night. I was delighted to find the watch and frustrated to see the bees still clustering in the tree as tight as a rugby ball but considerably larger.

My friend the minister arrived before the morning was out. 'Let me take over where you left off,' he suggested, 'and then you can come and be in at the death when we bring that swarm home!' Very reluctantly I agreed. In the evening we brought the swarm home in triumph. It was still raining quite heavily and the swarm was more than ready to be housed. I was building my apiary fast. The honey harvest was good. I gave away jar upon jar of honey. We had honey cakes and honey on our bread. I made mead. I brewed a gallon and then another. Mead need not be the heavy drink most people imagine it must be. It can be sweet or dry, light or heavy. It is the nearest thing to the product of the grape that man can make. It depends upon the flavour of the honey of the year in which it is brewed. It can make a man very muddle-headed. Brewed from nothing but yeast, honey and water, it is a very pure drink and I can well understand its popularity in the Middle Ages.

This year I have made five gallons of mead and two of muscatel mead, that is a brew of our own muscatel grapes, which have a strong and distinct flavour, sweetened only with honey. Only a beekeeper can be so extravagant, of course. The best honey is quite expensive and isn't often simply used to sweeten a brew or even to make a cake. Most imported honey is inferior in flavour to our own and the general public really doesn't know the taste of fresh honey any more than they know the new-laid egg of the free-range hen. This is no one's fault, of course, for honey that travels a long way undergoes changes in temperature or becomes thick through refrigeration. Eggs take days to pass from the hands of the producer to the retailer, to say nothing of another time lag when a wholesaler is involved. So few things are really fresh and uncontaminated that the words fresh and pure are generally misused.

I like honey on my bread. I like to crack a new-laid egg into a half pint of fresh milk, tip in a tablespoonful of fresh honey, and whip it all up in the blender to make a sweet, nourishing drink such as man knew a thousand years ago when he laboured to cultivate things for his own table. I am caught up in beekeeping. I don't know how many hives I will have by the time I draw the line— nor do I know what I will do with all the honey. These are bridges to be crossed when I come to them!

9

Duck-Keeper

KEEPING a hawk had involved daily chores and more, the exercising of the bird, but I had been tied down in a similar way when keeping sheep. The sheep had exercised me, running about to keep them in and provide them with food. The quails had tied me down, although not quite so much. Bees meant work in high summer, in autumn, and in spring again when they need feeding or cleaning out, but ducks? Didn't they just waddle about and eat grass and the occasional handful of barley? The friend who urged me to take on the overspill of his muscovy duck breeding—he was knee-deep in ducks and didn't know where to turn—said they ate grass. All he gave them when they wanted more was bread! They love that steamed bread that looks like cotton wool and tastes worse, he said. I looked at the waddling muscovies and thought how nice they would look on the green slope of the little orchard. The muscovy is short-legged, low-slung. It bumps its way over the slightest obstacle. Its feet are very large. I suppose in its native place it walks a great deal over mudbanks and needs large feet to support its heavy body. The drake is almost as big as a goose and I believe the species actually owes more to the goose tribe than the duck. Colouring varies from snow white to black and the male's beak is crusted with a brilliant

red that extends from the upper mandible to his forehead.
He looks aware of himself as a male. He hisses and raises
the feathers on his head when excited or alarmed, as does
the much smaller female. I accepted a duck and three
ducklings. We were fascinated by them. I put them in
what has become the 'duck shed', a space under the old
hawk house, walled on three sides by large slate slabs.
They seemed very happy below the hawk house. I put
a metal gate frame across the entrance and covered this
with weld-mesh, cutting out some of the grid-squares to
make a small exit or entrance for the duck brood. Now
they were securely housed I could close them in at night
and admire them on the grass by day.

My enthusiasm for ducks took hold. When I was
offered another duckling I accepted without hesitation.
I forgot only one thing. The three ducklings I already
had had been grouped with the duck. They were not her
offspring, but they had all been long enough together
to have become a unit dominated by the older duck. Now,
when I eagerly popped the newcomer in with his brothers
and sisters, the duck rejected him. She attacked him so
vigorously that I had fears for his survival. Blood streamed
from his head. I had to intervene. A day or so afterwards,
finding him crouched down and bleeding again, I decided
that I would have to find some way of integrating this
duckling with his former family. I separated the older
bird from the rest and all was peace and harmony. The
next thing to do was to bring the duck back to the young
ones, I said. I had hardly done so than I found a trail
of duck feathers leading to the hedge. The new duckling
had been driven out. He had decided to walk away!
I could find no other sign of him anywhere. I looked over
the adjoining property. Between my ground and my
neighbours there is a footpath, an old lane. The duckling
could have flapped through the hedge, dropped into the
lane, hurried on into the blackthorns, and found a way
over the wall into the jungle of brambles and young

sycamores beyond. How would I ever find him when he had had a considerable start and the area into which he had gone consists of about five acres? The fox would have him, I said. I was depressed, but I still had four ducks. They would grow and breed, or inbreed, in due course.

Days passed and then my son was stopped by a boy who lives down below. Could I tell him how to feed and look after a duck he had been given when it strayed into the kitchen of a house in the town? My duck that walked away seemed to have some instinct for the right place to go! He had been well-fed and handed over to the youngster concerned. This journey must have involved all kinds of hazards, crossing the path of the fox and a dog or two to say nothing of the traffic on the roads. The bird was a survivor if ever there was one.

'Tell the boy he has my muscovy duckling. I would like to have it back,' I said, my mind working on the problem as I spoke, 'and tell him that in exchange I will give him a full-grown duck.'

The duckling was brought back. After a bit of chasing and flapping and hissing the mother duck was cornered and put in a box and taken away. The duckling joined the rest of the family and was at peace among them. I took note of his behaviour after that. It was no ordinary duck. It was resourceful, enterprising, a born leader of its fellows and I was very glad to have it.

Muscovies take about four months to become full-sized. They moult a snowfall of white feathers and emerge looking as though they had been newly-painted. At rest they might be white boats moored in a harbour. Some people say the muscovy is an ugly, ungainly duck, but those who keep them grow to love them and see them as beautiful. I spent an hour in the morning watching them as they waddled in line up the steep slope of the garden, always in the same order, the resourceful drake at the head of the column of four. Only now and again did they change and walk line-abreast. I could imagine the leader giving the order 'Halt! Left turn! Quick march!' as they halted, turned and changed formation to come across the slope instead of waddling uphill. I was always met by this line when I went up to feed them bread or barley but I was always concerned to give them something better than bread. Bread contains little that will bring a duck into prime condition and put a sheen on its feathers. I fed barley and chopped-up greenstuff. When they came through the winter I put a couple of bales of hay into their shed thinking to give them some privacy when they began to lay. I didn't know my ducks then. There would be no laying in the shed as my father's sometime Khaki Campbells had done. The muscovy, which incidentally isn't a muscovite but a duck with a distinctive musk odour about it, likes to nest in isolated places, like the wild mallard. Like the mallard in captivity it is necessary to pinion the bird or it will fly off.

My little company was showing signs of stretching their wings. They would come out in the morning and go through a comic bowing display towards one another and then flap off like an inventor of the 18th or 19th century experimenting with devices to make him airborne. The muscovies did more than experiment. They became airborne. They flew in widening half-circles to crash-land on the grass. I knew that soon they would exercise their wing muscles to an extent that would make them capable of flying over the shires but I kept them in one morning and, with apologies to each one, I clipped a wing with a pair of scissors. It made me sad to see how the birds looked up at the crossing mallard and the pair of shelduck that always come to the clifftop in spring, seeking a nesting site they never find. Now the muscovies were earthbound I reproached myself. They hadn't deserved such callous treatment. If the fox came down they wouldn't be able to escape by taking to the air. He would almost certainly corner them and kill them.

By March the first duck was laying. I discovered this

by accident when, after I had let them out, I went back
to put some feed in the trough. It doesn't take long to
count three. Where was the fourth? The fourth was
nowhere to be found! I searched diligently. I reported
to the family that the fox had taken one of my ducks.
I was glooming about this when I looked out of the
window and counted four on the grass. There was an
explanation, but I didn't discover it until the following
morning. Again I could see only three ducks but this
time, instead of searching, I sat down and kept a careful
watch to discover the direction from which the missing
bird would come back for breakfast. To my surprise the
duck emerged from behind a sheet of corrugated iron
lying against the bole of a wych elm. In the space between
the tree trunk and the iron there was a stony cavity and
the duck had made this comfortable by plucking her
feathers to serve as a nest-lining. There were two ivory-
coloured eggs larger than the egg of a farmyard duck or a
mallard. That duck went on laying—ten eggs, twelve
eggs, sixteen. At eighteen, when she could no longer
cover them all, she stopped laying and began to incubate.

A farmyard duck will take a week longer than the
average hen to incubate her eggs. How long would the
muscovy take? I didn't know, and no one at hand could
tell me. It seemed that duck was going to sit forever.
In the meantime I found a second nest. Two of the three
ducks were laying and incubating. The third didn't seem
to have matured. Thirty-six eggs being brooded! I could
see that soon I would have a problem in duck husbandry,
but my immediate concern was for the sitting birds. How
to prevent the fox from scenting them, killing them and
devouring the eggs? It would have been useless to set
the partly-incubated eggs under a broody hen when the
average broody hen doesn't remain broody long enough.
Duck eggs are best incubated by a machine if the bird
itself doesn't sit. I asked the keeper what he would do.
We agreed that the duck would probably refuse to have

anything to do with her clutch if I moved her. The only way to fool the fox was to spoil the scent with something much stronger than the muscovy odour, creosote, tar, engine oil. I filled a milk bottle with tar oil which I use for spraying fruit trees. The smell persists for months. It is almost impossible to remove from clothes that are inadvertently sprayed or contaminated by the stuff. Many washings are involved if the wind changes and the spray chances to be blown back onto one's face. I 'dripped' a sort of magic circle round each duck nest. The fox didn't discover what it was all about. If he sniffed the air he went on and I steadily crossed off the days to find out how long a muscovy sits. A goose takes a little longer than a muscovy, but the muscovy needs thirty-six days before she walks off with her brood in tow. All at once it happened—there on the path was the mother duck. Flowing after her, stumbling and staggering, were sixteen little yellow ducklings! I don't think I have ever seen anything that delighted me so much.

'Come and see!' I shouted. The family came and watched.

It was a moving sight. The mother duck was proud of her brood. The sun shone but it was cold. April was upon us, but the wind blew from the snowy peaks of the distant mountains. There was a bleakness about the sunlight even when it touched the slope and illuminated the ducklings and made them seem golden.

That first day I found the duck trying to shelter her massive brood under her stretched wings but she wouldn't be shepherded into the shed. She quacked panic when I tried to gather her youngsters and lure her into the hawk hut and I had to abandon the gathering in. The next day two ducklings perished. I thought it might be something to do with the need for antibiotics. Young turkey chicks can go down like flies, and breeders are careful to make sure that they are fed the right sort of food and given the right medication. I hurried off and

got some special food. The death role was lengthening.
By the end of a week, even though I had at last gathered
the duck and her brood into the shelter of the long greenhouse, the last of the sixteen died. I was deflated, defeated,
and not at all encouraged when the second duck came
walking down the slope from the wood, where she too,
had brought off sixteen of her eighteen eggs. To have
ensured the survival of the second brood I would have
had to construct a brooder incorporating some kind of
heater, such as a pig-lamp, and kept the duck and her
ducklings under it from the outset. As it was I thought
about making a brooder when it was too late. The second
hatch of ducklings perished in exactly the same number
of days. They had all died from exposure. We should
have eaten the eggs as they were laid!

Muscovies are not easily daunted. They will rear a
second brood. Second broods began about six weeks later.
The weather was much warmer. The same nests were
used and hardly had the original two birds begun to sit
than the third found a place she liked down in the hedge-
bottom where she contented herself with twelve eggs
before she began to incubate. Now, counting my ducklings before they were hatched, I saw myself with at least
forty. I knew now that the weather wouldn't kill them off.
I also knew that in another year I would prevent the first
eggs from being incubated and avoid the tragedy that
had befallen the ducks this season. My diary contained
all the information I needed to predict when the little
orchard would be over-run by ducklings. In the course
of time we had three broods, a total of thirty ducklings.
The second clutches had a slightly lower fertility rate
and the duck in the hedge-bottom brought off the
smallest brood. Now it was plain that the mother of a
brood recognised every member of it and was hostile
to the offspring of her sisters. This was not at all amusing
for the attack upon the innocent duckling that didn't
know its own family from its cousins was fierce and

merciless. I had to do what I could to isolate the brood
with the longest gap in hatching for they, being the
smallest birds, suffered most. The other two ducks kept
themselves to themselves and led their broods to different
grazing places, avoiding the clashes which marked the
early days. It was almost autumn before all three groups
of young ducks were assimilated into one. I had quite a
problem now, for the shed was crowded. I also needed a
vast amount of barley to keep the flock well fed.

What now? I asked myself. If I brought something
like thirty-five ducks through the winter and they began
to breed in the spring we would soon have to move away
to make room for them! People round about would
protest if I allowed them to fly and feed on their barley
fields. The whole thing might get out of hand. A friend
said I could have roast duckling every day if I could only
kill them, but I had grown so fond of this flock of ducks
that I couldn't bear the thought of killing them, let alone
eating them. They followed me about and fed from my
fingers, jumping up for morsels of food like performing
seals and standing *en masse*, their beaks half-open in
anticipation whenever I approached the place in which
they were feeding.

'Good boys, good boys,', I would tell them, and they
would all make a breathless sound that was intended to
let me know they wanted some further mark of my favour,
a crust, some barley, some chopped-up cabbage.

It isn't easy to give ducks away when one exacts a
promise from anyone offering to take them that they will
be preserved, looked after and not betrayed and slaugh-
tered. I hesitate to say how many ducks I have killed in my
day, how many I have stopped in mid-air with a shotgun
and watched them crumple and thump to the ground or
go planing down into the rushes of the marsh. I confess
to having killed far too many, and too often. Now, when
I approached the giving-away of my flock of ducks I
admitted that I was a sentimentalist about them. I really

loved the performers, the muster of black and white ducks that greeted me every morning, rain or shine. They had only come to be fed, of course, but they trusted me so that I could grab one and pick it up and it would cock an eye at me and wonder what had come over me. I could hold my cupped palms and have a dozen ducks all jostling to feed from them at once. Whoever received them would have to have a feeling for them.

The first friend who showed a genuine interest said he knew about ducks and regarded them as more intelligent and much greater characters in their own right than any mere backyard fowl. He would take a dozen if I cared to part with so many. I was delighted. I talked to another friend, the Forest Warden. He readily agreed to have a batch on a secluded forest lake. A third friend would take some and I would be left with seven, the perfect number. There was only one remaining hurdle. I had to bring myself to the parting. I put off the day or days when the flock would be divided up into families and distributed among those who would give them food and shelter. I looked at my morning parade and it saddened me. The ducks were unaware that I had the power and the will to break up their group and confront them with a different existence to the one they enjoyed in my care. I was even a little ashamed to think that I took such a right over them!

At last, having fashioned a crate, I telephoned the first friend and said I would break the group and give him his 'family' as soon as he gave me notice of his intended arrival. He came a few days later and I crated a dozen birds. After that it was easy. The second batch went. My mass parade of ducks was at an end. The others seemed to look upon me with less trust now. They hissed and showed their crests, nervous of my approach. It wasn't until the final batch had been carted off that the final seven settled down to feed from my hands again. I missed the flock. I saw the seven as individuals. They quickly settled down and went to roost in the shed, which, since the days of the nesting and hatching of broods, I no longer fastened up at night. In the mornings the seven were always out grazing when I got up. I suppose they fed in the night, for ducks have an instinct for nocturnal activity. It would be enough to breed from the remaining birds, if I ever wanted another flock, I told myself. The seven consisted of four drakes and three ducks. This imbalance was due to the fact that I failed to recognise the drakes as they developed. Now, when I could do nothing about it, I found I had more drakes than I would ever need.

The Forest Warden telephoned me with reports of the settling in of his flock. They were being hand-fed on the lake. Everything went well until all at once a count revealed that there had been a casualty. The fox had discovered the innocents, the pinioned duck that couldn't escape him when he got between them and the water's edge. A second casualty followed almost at once. This is the way of the fox in winter. He returns to the place where he gets an easy kill. The Warden hastily made a survey of his area and brought the flock away from the lake to a pen with a pool on a stream, a place that was fox-proofed. I was depressed about this and amused when another friend reported that his flock seemed to be about to depart. One had flown off and fed on the estuary. The others would follow perhaps? I seemed to have forgotten to mention that my wing-trimming had been minimal and by now the duck would need further attention, but the wanderer returned and it and its brothers and sisters were quickly pinioned.

In the meantime, having gone in for hens, bantams and golden pheasants, it was my habit to go up to the little orchard each evening at dusk and lock up the hens. I didn't bother to close up the ducks. What followed was inevitable and tragic! The fox came.

Long ago there was a fox that plagued the area. It was shot on our boundary. It was an old, mangy fox that had operated by day and he was killed in an ambush. The fox that came down to the ducks had been lying out on our cliff for a long time. I had seen his tracks and he had left his card along the way. Once I had had a brief glimpse of him as he went up through the wood and caught a whiff of his strong smell as he made off at top speed. I had forgotten him. Foxes don't often kill on their own doorstep.

On the night he came down it was quite cold. I was glad to sit close to the fire and have my supper on a tray on my knees until the telephone rang. Someone enquired if we had lost a duck. By this time I was wellknown as a keeper of ducks just as I had been wellknown as a keeper of hawks of different sorts. Even my bees advertised us. They would swarm over the wall when I was taking honey and sting anyone in the lane on the other side, although I always denied that the offenders were mine! Had I lost a duck? No, I was sure of that. I sat a while thinking after I had put the telephone down. Just as well go and count heads, I told myself. I put on my boots, took a torch, and went up to look into the shed. I was dismayed when I could see only two rather frightened ducks perched on the top of the hay bale. Five missing! This couldn't be. The duck someone had seen heading for town was obviously one of my seven. What had driven them out? I asked myself the question and tried not to think of the obvious answer. At that moment I caught sight of something white lying in the middle of the young apple trees. I rushed over and found a drake. He was quite dead. His neck had been nipped and the killing had been expertly done by the fangs of the fox! What a fine handsome fellow he had been only an hour ago. He was still warm. Where were the others? I cast about with the torch and found a second drake. He stood behind some wire-netting with his wings drooping and blood pouring down his arched neck. Poor fellow, he looked as though he hadn't long to live. He tried to get away when I reached for him and brought him out from behind the netting which had undoubtedly discouraged the fox from going in for the kill. Placed on his feet, the poor bird dropped its wings and stood motionless. I took him to the shed and put him inside. I was filled with remorse at not having closed the place. I began to think of the birds still unaccounted for. A fox couldn't carry them all off. One down in the town? There might be another there, even three in all. Could the fox have been disturbed and gone off after failing to kill one drake and killing the one I had picked up among the apple trees? I hurried down to the cottage to break the news of disaster and had hardly got there when I met the boy to whom I had given the duck when the whole business began. He was carrying my missing drake. Two ducks remained to be accounted for now. I made a tour of the immediate area. I called on the police in town and asked them to be good enough to contact me if anyone reported a duck. The information was recorded after I had clarified it. The police were more used to requests for information about missing dogs. They had never been asked to look out for a duck, although they had seen a fox ambling through town in the middle of the night.

I went back home and made another search. In the farthermost corner of the garden, head-first in a cavity between a wall and a piece of sheet iron, I found one of the two missing ducks. The other duck had gone, however. I looked again at daylight but the whole thing was quite hopeless. The fox had left only a feather or two but he had carried one of the ducks up the cliff and, unless I strengthened my defences, he would be back. A fox can only be a fox. It is no use blaming him for being a predator although I can't understand what makes him kill more than once and leave victims he can't carry away. I suppose the keeper would have tracked him with his terriers, dug him out and killed him, but I hadn't time for that. I knew, in any case, that a fox kills like this when the ground is hard and cold weather makes it impossible for him to find other prey. Rats, mice, insects are deep in the ground. Birds roost high and in the bare wood they can see him as he tries to approach. He haunts places where there is a chance of catching a straying hen, a Christmas duck or the traditional goose. I once came upon a lying-out place of a fox with the remains of a fine fat goose strewing the ground. I suppose my poor duck was chewed up somewhere in the gorse or the thorn thickets up above. Now I would have to make everything doubly secure. I would lock away the ducks at evening and never give the fox another chance.

I mourned the dead ducks and kept an eye on the poor fellow who had been so badly mutilated. Neither he nor the other four would come out of the shed for two days. The shock had seriously affected them. The injured one didn't eat for almost a week. His neck seemed permanently crooked. His head was askew and he would sit for long intervals with his eyes closed. It might have been kinder to have made an end of him, and I seriously considered doing so. There was, however, a very slight improvement in the way he moved and at last he emerged with the others and waddled up to take a drink and a little barley. He found swallowing difficult. He appeared very tame but I discovered that it pained him even to waddle away.

Day by day the invalid improved. The blood on his neck had congealed and dried. He bathed himself in the drinking dish and looked a little better. The wound healed. Feathers began to grow. His beak had turned pale and his plumage had lost its lustre, but slowly he showed improvement. Soon he could face the others and look after himself. He had sat all day by himself, enjoying the occasional spell of sunshine. Now he came hurrying to be fed and at last he was able to take crusts from my fingers again.

I am inclined to think the fox came every night for

quite a while. Now I see no sign of him but locking up is a ritual that must continue.

I began with five ducks. I still have five. I don't think I shall breed another flock. I know the ways of muscovies. If I had a flock I would have to keep their bath/pond full of water. For a while I did this and had to rescue the foolish hens that fell in and couldn't get out again, but that is another story. One thing has happened that I didn't bargain for when it all began. I have ceased to be a wildfowler. I have become too fond of ducks to think of shooting them, whatever sort they may be. It is perhaps late in the day for a man to change when he has passed his middle age, but better late than never. I might examine myself and say it is an emotional thing, but I am not quite sure that it is entirely so. I wouldn't shoot the fox in cold blood. I didn't go and try to find him. I even understood him taking a duck on a cold winter's night. I just wish he had chosen someone else's duck, a duck that wasn't involved with its owner or vice versa!

10

Bantams and Battery Birds

Beware of Pity was the title of a book by Stefan Zweig, a great writer who understood what compassion means, although his study of the subject in a most brilliant novel didn't extend to hens! I was talking to a farmer friend when he suggested I might be interested in buying some birds culled from the battery. They were just past their peak performance on the production line, he said. They would be ideal for storing in the deep freeze. I could have a dozen or two if I cared to call and collect them. The price was almost nominal. I decided that I would have a dozen, imagining that I could keep them in the old pigeon house at the far end of our bit of ground, kill them off and pluck them over a period of days, and consign them to the deep freeze until such time as we felt like having a broiler for dinner. This was the plan. Everyone agreed that it was reasonable, rational and practical in every way.

I drove off to the farm and the battery house to collect my fat hens. The man in charge of them went along the row of prison cells like the governor on inspection, except that he carried a sack dangling from one hand. When he came to a bird he felt might be culled he reached into the cage, pulled it out, flapping and protesting, and pushed it into the sack. One, two, three, he counted.

I carried away the first sackful and came back for the second. The battery house was only dimly lit, but full of the sound of cackling hens and eggs rolling down from the heroines of the production line as they achieved their norm. There was a suggestion of dust and powdered pellets drifting in the air, a dry atmosphere, but the gloom obscured horror. I didn't appreciate how the inmates really looked until I had my two sacks of condemned prisoners away from their Sing-Sing galleries.

The combs of the hens were grey. They were without feathers from their heads to their underbellies! Worse still, their claws were bleeding for these had grown round the wires of the cages and the hens had had to be pulled out forcibly. They hadn't stretched a leg since they had gone into the cell as 'point-of-lay' pullets. They had lived in the gloom for nearly a year, drinking water and feeding through the bars of the cage. Their droppings, falling through the bottom of the cage, had been brushed and scraped away and the place periodically treated with disinfectant. I stared at the pathetic creatures as they huddled on the floor of the pigeon house, where, despite the fact that I had put up perches, they had to remain until they were killed off if they didn't manage to flap up to roost. They couldn't stand. When they did, they toppled against the wall of the house. They looked like old women overcome by too much gin. I knew, even as I regarded them in the light of my torch, that I couldn't eat them. They didn't look healthy but it wasn't that. I was so sorry for the wretched creatures that I determined to rehabilitate them. I would keep them until their feathers grew, until their combs were red and they could walk on the grass of the orchard, lie on their sides and take a dust bath! I closed the door on them and went away with a slight anxiety that the change from a temperature-controlled battery might result in chills which would kill them off in a couple of days.

In the morning they were all clustered together in one

corner of the house. I fed them. They picked at the food I
scattered, swaying on weak legs and crouching to get at
the pellets I had thrown on the floor. I opened the door
and let them see that they could venture outside but they
had never been outside. The air was cold. The world was
full of unusual sounds and the light far stronger than
they had known. They peered beyond the open door.
I thought of miners coming up after a shift underground.
But what a sight they were! One had a hooked beak that
made it impossible for her to pick up the pellets. How
she had fared in the battery I couldn't imagine.

One of the tattered company had laid a fine, large
brown egg. I took it down to the cottage, knowing that
the change would affect them all. I couldn't expect them
to lay but I could expect casualties if I kept them.

The first casualty came when one of the group managed
to flap up and perch. She crouched on the board. I was
encouraged to think that soon the others would roost,
although their flight feathers had been clipped to fit the
cage, or had worn away as they developed in that confined
space. The perched bird flew down next morning and
dislocated both thigh bones. I knew she would never
stand up again. Those that had crouched on the floor
seemed to have gained a little strength. They tottered
out to inspect the run. They were nervous and would
have injured themselves flapping back into the house had
I not made a gangplank way for them. It rained, a soft,
light rain which matted their feathers and made the birds
look even worse than they had done when I brought them
home. I began to feel the whole thing was hopeless and I
might as well make a quick and humane end of them all—
bury them in the garden. The thought was underlined
when the poor old thing with the dislocated legs simply
drooped her head and died where she sat in a box of hay.
I took her broken body away and buried it where nothing
could unearth it. One of the others limped. She had
strained her foot. The egg-layer gave up laying of course

for the chain of ovary production had halted. I was now running a hospital for sick birds.

In a matter of a couple of weeks I began to see an improvement. The missing feathers on the rubbed parts of the bodies of the birds began to be replaced by small quills. Their combs remained grey but their eyes brightened. The nervousness out of doors diminished and the 'old ladies' would cluster round me to be fed. When I talked to them they cocked their heads and listened. I felt that what I had was a geriatric ward of pensioned-off hens but my affection for them grew day by day. I had never known tamer birds. I suppose I was the first person who had ever treated them with kindness. They loved the freedom of the grass. Each day they covered a slightly wider area until I would find them running to meet me from all points of the compass. They walked with me, not when I came to feed them, but anytime I went up to see that they were well. I would turn abruptly downhill, and we would all go downhill, turn right, and the company gently promenaded in that direction. I was aware that I represented something more than their warder in prison. They were led by me but I held out my arms to shepherd them into the run and they obediently went in before me. I put them into the house with ease. They welcomed me in the morning with a crooning sound and every day I noticed that they were getting stronger and more like the birds of the paddocks of my childhood, the birds no one ever thought to call free-range hens until someone thought to make prisoners of them.

Don't let the professional poultry keeper, the master of the battery and his wardens, say I don't know the cost of producing an egg, or the problem of meeting the demand. I know all the excuses for treating animals as though man is God's beloved son, capable of no evil and put upon the earth to use all other forms of life as he likes. The consumer is the criminal, it is said. The producer fills the need. The same excuse might be made by the keeper of a brothel, although the indecency of the battery is mitigated by the fact that the birds are never cold, never wet, fed vitamins, minerals and water. A happy hen lays, they say. An unhappy bird wouldn't lay! The pale yolk was a drawback to the business, but yolks are no longer pale. The scientist solved this problem. In semi-darkness no one notices or comments upon the grey comb, the over-grown claws and beaks, the eternal crouch of the bird literally hooked to the grid. We need eggs. We demand chicken rough, frozen chicken, broilers. Where would such things come from and who would pay the market price, if sentimentalists had their way and the battery, or the factory farm, producing barley beef, had to be closed down?

Conscience is a convenient thing. What the eye doesn't see the mind doesn't grieve over. We live walled out from truth and reality. Steak isn't part of an animal and milk comes from bottles. Eggs are packed in see-through, egg-shaped containers. We prefer them brown, of course, and pay a penny or two more for that. We know the frozen chicken but we see the same bird with feathers less frequently than we see pigeons in the square or sparrows on the roof. The battery bird exists, as we know poverty and misery exist, but we don't like to think of sordid things when we are consulting the menu asking what our guests thinks of the item headed Chicken—*suprême de volaille*, *à la crème*, *à la Kiev* or *chasseur*. Who would choose chicken *bastille*?

If my collection of hens continued to make progress I might see them resplendent and full-feathered by early summer, but they still had a long way to go. They still crouched. I had to trim their claws so that they could scratch the earth and walk without hobbling. I found them resting like loungers against walls. I gave them greenstuff to eat. I scattered their food in the long grass and made them exercise themselves to find it. I watched them drink raindrops and fluff out their feathers, lumber

after butterflies and now and again make a capture of one.
I was delighted when a particularly smart hen seized a
mouse which she ambled away to devour on her own,
harassed for most of the way by her curious and envious
sisters. The world had changed for these brown hens.
I was as happy to see them enjoying the sunshine as they
were basking in it.

There had never been a pecking order in prison
because the birds had lived just out of reach of one
another, but now, herded together, going up to roost—
the last of them had given up crouching on the floor—
an order of precedence had come to operate. There were
dominant hens and dominated hens. Little set-to's had
established who had priority. The bolder characters
picked first and the order was generally respected even
though lower in the hierarchy there were occasional
contests to settle the matter. Fat hens with hackles up
would confront one another for minutes on end, striking
out like fat boys fighting, but rarely drawing blood. The
group was nervous of the muscovy ducks. The muscovy
drake was aware that hissing brought the boldest of the
hens to an indignant halt. The barley trough was for
ducks. That must be understood! The sunken bath was
also for ducks, but the hens had never seen anything so
attractive, and one or two, flapping wildly, skidded over
the porcelain edge and tried to swim. I rescued them
again and again. They were none the worse for their
immersion but I knew that each time if I hadn't happened
along at the right moment they would have drowned.
So the ducks lost their miniature pond and had to give
themselves a stand-up bath at the drinking vessels. It was
generally over water that the contests between the brown
hens and the ducks took place. Soon, when their combs
had become red and their necks fully feathered, the
hens faced up to the red-beaked, hissing drake with his
crest raised. They boldly drove him back until he was
intimidated. He would even retreat from the feeding

trough. When the hens came rushing from the run on their release in the morning they hurried like overweight matrons rushing to a sale, or trying to catch a bus.

By the time the ducks were incubating their eggs I started to find the occasional hen's egg. The outcasts from the battery started to lay without their carefully weighed ration, without the temperature-controlled building and the water drip. They produced an egg every day, every one of them! I thought about this later on when there was a power cut. It seemed to me that the production line means something more than an egg a day. It probably means an egg in 23 hours—something more than 365 eggs in a year, although the bird may not be kept for this long. This may be the secret the producer doesn't reveal when he talks about rhythm, light, temperature and efficiency. Birds that are free to wander use energy and are distracted. They get chilled. They may miss a day. Five hundred birds missing one laying day in six months is unthinkable. The lapse can hardly be tolerated when the accountant sits on his stool carefully working out the cost of production, depreciation, replacement, even the value of manure as well as the carcass price obtained at the broiler factory. The power cuts disrupted the laying cycles of countless batteries throughout the country. A loss was written into every balance sheet! My refugees still didn't miss a day and went on laying, although I must admit that it had taken two to three months to restore them to health and used to an out-of-doors, free existence. No market producer could have permitted himself such indulgence or would have forgotten for a minute that profit is the thing that makes the world go round, even if a rich man may find it hard to enter the kingdom of heaven.

By midsummer I found that the necks and backs of my battery birds had a positive sheen, a brilliance that was quite arresting. Everyone who saw them stood and

admired them and asked how I had achieved such
condition in such poor birds. The truth was that these
were most carefully bred birds of the finest strain. They
were enjoying insects, seeds, balanced food, sunshine,
fresh air. They glowed with health. They laid the finest
eggs because they were a selected laying strain. I exulted
in their beauty. I only occasionally thought that they
would one day cease to lay and grow old. I promised
myself that they would never be put down, but end their
days naturally. I would care for them and feed them
because I had become even more involved with them
than with my flock of sheep. How could it be otherwise
when, walking along the path back from the hen-run, one
of these fat, red-brown hens would croon at me and 'talk'
to me as she fell into step and accompanied me to the
gate? Like someone slightly out of his wits I would make
clucking sounds to the hen and she would hold a conversation with me. Dear me, I sometimes said when I
got indoors, I wish, like Konrad Lorenz, I could master
the language of birds. We are only a hair's breadth from
communication. I wish I had Mr Lorenz's unself-
consciousness and deep understanding of birds to
encourage me to persist and communicate. One day we
may achieve this, although it may come much too late
to make any difference to the awful thing mankind in
general condones—the changing of all domestic animals
into machines.

My flock of eleven has already had more than a year
of life beyond the expectation of battery birds. There
have been times when I felt I should go back and rescue
another batch of hens from the battery or the broiler
factory, but the whole business would be like trying to
row up Niagara Falls. Where would it end? How could
I find the means to repair the ravages of the production
line and see that all the miserable inmates of all the
batteries in Britain ended their days in peace on the green
field? The thing is a sentimentalist's dream. It can't be

done. Besides, the interests of the producer are well presented wherever criticism is made before legislators or officials of societies concerned. The treatment of battery hens, animals like pigs and bullocks, even the horse, about which more people wax sentimental than almost all domestic animals save the dog, will continue to disgrace man until he is better educated and civilised. It was this way with the treadmill dog churning butter, or turning the spit, the sport of bear-baiting or cock-fighting.

Not going back for more battery hens was excusable. I lacked accommodation for more. I had simultaneously embarked upon another long-cherished dream—to keep bantams. Being already tied down with ducks I might as well be tied down with bantams, I told myself. I had a romantic dream about the dwarf hen. I could remember them in my childhood, those neat little birds that picked their way around the door of the blacksmith's cottage and sat sunning themselves under his flowering currant bush. My grandfather had kept bantams, too. I had a nostalgic longing to keep them. The bantam, the cottager's laying hen, the little bird with the nest in the nettlebed or the bramble bush or the shrill crowing cock as brave as anything twice his size, is hard to find nowadays. I made enquiries here and there and managed to locate three. They were of the bantam breed, although not of a name-able variety—Rosecomb, Black Pekin, Spangled Game, Millefleur, Barbus or Maran. I had to be content with crossbreds or mongrels, for only the competition breeder keeps the pure strains. After discovering three hens in one place I managed to obtain three more in another, and then another three. They seemed even more 'miniature' when I looked at them and at the great, fluffed out, red battery hens whose feet were enormous. I wanted more than nine hens. I needed a cockerel. I made repeated enquiries for a cock. With a mixed lot of birds from different sources I could breed my own little birds. All that remained to do then was to amalga-

mate the flock, introduce the dwarf hens to the henhouse
in which the big hens lived.

The cock I obtained was accompanied by a bird
slightly smaller than he was. They were almost perfect
Rosecombs, jet black with the neat build of this variety.
The cock began to crow almost at once. Alas, his 'sister'
turned out to have been mis-sexed. I had two cockerels
and, after a few weeks, twice as much crowing to awaken
me in the morning! I had had another life-long wish, to
awaken to the cockcrow. The crowing of cocks may
irritate some people, but it delights me. It harks back to
the days when I was small and cocks crowed to the
morning sun long before it was up over the rim of the
distant hills. I would lie awake in my attic bedroom and
the sound made me so happy that sometimes tears would
come to my eyes. Now the cocks crowed, vieing with one
another. They never stopped crowing. The clarion call
of the bantam cock lacks a little of the bass note of the
ordinary, full-sized bird. It is more shrill. The sound is
made much more frequently. My wife complained that
she was having too much of a good thing. I could lie in
bed and sigh for my happy childhood as much as I liked,
but enough was enough! I must move the cockerels
farther away. I complied. The flock of bantams was
transferred after dark in a couple of sacks and popped
in with the battery birds. The little ones weren't a bit
overawed by the bulk of the big hens. They flapped up
and perched, but kept themselves to themselves at first.
The cocks crowed in the night and the frequency of their
crowing progressed with the coming of daylight. In the
morning I hurried up and let the flock out. The big hens
kept to themselves. The bantams likewise stayed together
and went off foraging in the hedgebottom, round the
gooseberry bushes and the derelict currant bushes.
Continual crowing advertised their content. I began to
search for nests, for they had been laying before they
were moved from the wired pen I had constructed near

the house. Finding laying-away bantams is an endless chore for the person who keeps these little hens. I searched high and low, and as quickly as I discovered a hidden nest the bird went off and found some new secret place. I would bring down two eggs, no eggs and then twelve eggs, discovering a nest in under a bush or behind a bit of corrugated iron. I walked through the long grass and the nettles and came upon a brooding bantam hen. She was picked up and isolated to sit in peace. In three weeks I had six little black chicks barely the size of a golf ball.

Broodiness is a natural thing in most naturally-raised hens although the whole flock may not become broody in the course of a season. The man who wants to raise chicks watches the broody bird and after it has settled down he gives it a selected clutch of eggs to incubate. One of the big red hens became broody, fluffed out her feathers and clucked her impatience with her sisters. I put her in a coop and set half a dozen bantam eggs beneath her, and then a second bantam showed the same symptoms. I set another clutch of eggs and then another. I was going to have a fair stock of bantams by the time I finished! The big red hen brought off her bantam chicks and seemed unaware that they were midgets. I noticed that she sometimes put her great foot on one and the poor little creature was flattened, but it recovered almost at once and the mother hen tucked it in under her ample mantle of feathers to shelter from the cold wind. I had chicks everywhere, it seemed. I was oblivious to the fact that some of them were bound to be cockerels. The multiplication of the flock intrigued me. I was surrounded by ducklings and soon I had almost as many little bantams.

When the brambles are ripe, they say, bantams cease to lay. The saying is based on fact. Quite abruptly the bantams went off the lay as autumn approached. A bird that incubates in the thunder storm loses most of her clutch. This too, I discovered, for one of the bantams had begun to sit on eggs in the long grass at the corner of the little orchard. I discovered her, wet and bedraggled, sitting tight while overhead thunder rolled and lightning flashed. Instead of the six chicks she might have brought off she hatched only one and that turned out to be a cockerel! I wondered about the balance of cocks and hens while the pullets were growing. I suppose I could have sexed them by the pendulum, which is an old-fashioned way of deciding which are cocks and which are hens in a company of half-grown or unfledged birds. Dangle a ring or a needle over the bird and the answer will be given by the object swinging to and fro or rotating. I watched the development of combs and wattles and congratulated myself on having sixty per cent hens. Self-congratulation was premature. The final result was almost fifty-fifty. Some of the birds were black, some attractive combinations of the marking of both parents. I couldn't rely on the sex-link rule, those favouring the male coloration being hens, and those looking more like the hen being cockerels because cross-breeding which had taken place in earlier generations made this an unreliable rule.

Soon I had nine cocks a-crowing and miniature hens hollowing out the path and dustbathing every few yards. The flock was integrated now, the big hens sharing perches and roosting corners with tiny bantams. The cockerels were making up to the enormous matrons with amorous approaches which the big hens didn't always accept. The cocks took time out from crowing to fight one another, going through a ritual of head lifting and lowering with hackles raised until I became almost as mesmerised as they were and then breaking off to leap up and strike, alight again and repeat the whole performance. Odd pairs spent all day doing this. Their brothers and sisters let them get on with it. I wondered whether I should keep some of the cocks and let them reach a ripe age so that I could use their capes—neck and head feathers—for fly-tying. Good cock hackles are scarce

and expensive to buy, more than a pound a cape, especially if the hackles happen to be distinctively marked or
coloured—furnace, for instance, coch-y-bonddu, grizzle,
honey dun or blue dun. This was a sort of let out.
I didn't want to kill the cockerels. I was involved with
them, every one. Although the books list even bantams
as layers or table birds, I hesitated at the thought of
wringing necks and making an end of birds I had seen
emerge from under the hen as tiny balls of fluff.

What happens to a person in my situation is a complete
change in nature and outlook. I had already come half
way with the sheep. I had been captivated by the ducks.
Now I was caught up by bantams and battery hens. They
had me, even although I couldn't pretend to be a Saint
Francis. A certain peace comes with this change in
outlook and the trust between man and beast flourishes.
I found that even blackbirds (which I had often stoned
out of the raspberry canes) came close to me. I had a
robin fly onto my hand one day and small birds accompanied me into the food store or into the henhouse. My
aura had changed, the mystic would say. I can't really
explain it but if a man's nature radiates in waves from his
subconscious, the message is well understood by all
animals.

Now, in the second winter of being husbandman to
ducks and hens, I haven't solved the problem of what to
do about the cockerels. At this moment, having given one
away and lost one through some mysterious malady
affecting only him, I have nine cockerels. One lives in
isolation and has been kept in a pen to be fattened for the
table for at least four weeks. I know that soon he will be
restored to the henhouse and join in the dawn crowing
with all the others. Hoppity, the lame hen, folds her
strained claws and plods along on the stump at great
speed. She, and eight of her sisters, still provide us with
eggs every day. Only two birds have stopped laying and I
feel sure even they will lay again this spring. The problem

of old age isn't upon the flock yet, although one or two of the original bantam stock are showing signs of age. They may serve as foster mothers should I allow the flock to expand in the early summer, as it did last year. I am tempted to construct another henhouse and keep more birds, ignoring the fact that hens don't pay. I don't keep them to make them pay. In fact, I give the eggs away to those in need of them and those who know what a fresh egg really is—an egg that isn't a month reaching the table.

My battery birds are like old friends. I know them well. They settle round my feet and nestle against me. They talk to me continually and I talk back. They begin to run towards me when I am fifty yards from the gate on the path. They walk with me even when I go up into the wood to look in at lay-away nests, and they always croon a welcome to me the minute they hear me approach the henhouse door in the morning. I suppose it all sounds a little mad to a strap-hanger on the London Underground, a civil servant on his way to Whitehall or a teacher in one of those outsized, glasshouse comprehensive schools. It may even sound a little mad to a psychiatrist. I have no way of deciding whether I am out of step with life and mankind, or whether the rest of the world is out of step with me and the reality of life and living. Not everyone can keep ducks, hens, bees and sheep to discover that all life is sacred. Not everyone would be at peace as I am now at peace with life even if it has taken me nearly sixty years to attain it! Nor am I finished with the formulation of my creed, far from it. I have much to learn, and mistakes to make, before I can charm the bird off the tree or walk in the company of the lion without fear.

II

Pursuit of Phantams

IT happened that when I was about to embark on keeping bantams a young friend came to me and asked if I would care to take on a pair of golden pheasants. The birds had been the cherished pets of an Irish labourer working on a contract in Liverpool. He had kept them in the backyard of a lodging house but, finding that the contract upon which he was working was about to end, he had had to make the decision to move on. There aren't many digs or lodging houses that will take a man with a dog, let alone a shrieking golden pheasant cock and the Irishman had called on my friend to ask if he could accommodate the pair of pheasants in his school. They would be something beautiful for the Liverpool slum boys to look at and admire. My friend had readily accepted the pair but there had been a drawback. The only suitable place to keep the pheasants was on the roof of the school where a pen was made for them. The birds walked to and fro in a run and looked out upon the foggy world of Merseyside. The air was far from clean. In a month the gold of the cock's crest had bleached to silver. The red of his breast and flanks had faded. He and his mate were suffering from the pollution. Some people think that pollution is in rivers and affects plant life without realising that it affects man himself. The golden pheasant might have been a warning signal to people in that part of the world. As it was, my friend decided that the birds could hardly survive another season in that atmosphere and brought them to me.

I must admit that they looked a sorry sight and far from my recollection of the golden pheasant that strolled proudly across the path of the 'big house' when I went to a garden fête there at the age of about three. I had never forgotten the startling magnificence of that bird and now the Liverpool birds almost disillusioned me. Had it all been a child's dream, part of the wonderland? I penned the two pheasants, gave them some shelter from the rain, carried in turf and generally did what I could to create a natural atmosphere. The cock was as restless as a caged tiger, darting up and down and to and fro. If he had ever been in the open before he had evidently forgotten. The hen was a little more stable and began to scrape and pick like a bantam. Lacking the splendid plumage of her mate, the golden pheasant hen is almost inconspicuous beside him. Both birds are smaller than the common pheasant hen although occasionally, because of cross-breeding somewhere along the line going back to the original imports from China, larger birds are encountered. My pair are of smaller dimensions, indicating, perhaps, a degree of inbreeding in the stock. Between bantam crowing and pheasant cry I knew that I had birds to be tended and looked after! The cock golden pheasant's cry rivals the screech of the Guinea fowl which some keepers stock to give warning of intruders in the cover. There are at least two wild golden pheasant cocks in the adjoining woods here although the keeper tells me he has no idea how such exotic pheasants got there. He is careful to warn the shooting parties not to fire upon them and the hardy golden pheasants continue to survive. They, incidentally, are bigger birds than the pair I have penned.

It amused me to see how the cock golden pheasant, whose colouring improved rapidly with proper feeding— at first egg yolk and biscuit, then a balanced pellet and a variety of seed—began to take an interest in the bantams. He would display his fine crest and mantle to impress them and sidle up to them making a shrill noise now and again. The bantams treated him with disdain. When they were all penned together he was sometimes heartily attacked and driven off for being a nuisance. He was never discouraged for long. His mate avoided the bantams altogether. She was fast on her legs and could swoop down to feed and return to the perch long before the bantams were aware that I had put some special morsel in the pen. The golden cock was always too busy showing off. Half his time I think he starved because he was a Lothario, a would-be Casanova among the bantam flock. In May while bantams were still in the pen I noticed that the golden pheasant hen was preparing to lay. She had made a half-hearted attempt to flatten a few strands of dead grass into a depression in a sheltered corner of the pen. Soon after this she laid her first egg and she went on laying on alternate days for the next two months. Some of the bantam eggs, I discovered, bore a close resemblance to the more pointed golden pheasant egg which is white and not fawny brown like the common pheasant's egg. I began to think about the cross that may result in the phantam.

Long ago, when my father lived here, there was great excitement when someone discovered a sort of half-chicken, half-pheasant bird running about in the bushes and undergrowth of the wood down below. Since Father kept hens it was assumed that this strange bird was a cross between a pheasant hen and one of Father's cockerels. On the other hand, it could have been some migrant ground bird strayed into the wood and remaining there. No one quite knew what to make of it. The odd bird was captured and brought up to the cottage but my mother was ill at that time and Father had more to do than study birds. He popped it into the hen-run where it managed to rush about and fend for itself despite the pursuit by hens who resented an intruder, but the inevitable happened. The outsider popped into the henhouse or was chased in there and cornered. Death was swift. Father discovered the tragedy when it was too late to decide what sort of bird it had been. He buried it and told me about it afterwards. Whether this bird was a pheasant-hen cross or a bantam-pheasant cross, which it could have been if someone in the vicinity had bantam cockerels free to mate with a wandering pheasant hen, I never found out. I wrote about the strange bird and as a result had some correspondence with a gentleman who had bred phantams. More than this, he claimed that the cross could be fertile and that second-generation breeding wasn't out of the question. The idea intrigued me. I promised myself that one day, when I had the time and the opportunity to do so, I would keep bantams and see whether I could produce a cross between them and a pheasant.

Every gamekeeper who uses bantams to incubate pheasant eggs knows that the bantam cock will mate with pheasant hens, and pheasant cocks, frustrated by the laying pheasant hens being screened off, will make up to any bantam hen. There is nothing new about this, but no one seems to know very much about the phantam which may result. I have considered the matter in the light of information offered by a number of people who know about natural selection and the attraction of one colour in particular. I believe that a golden pheasant cock, for instance, will mate more readily with a bantam hen that resembles the golden pheasant hen, a brown-fawn, speckled bird of slight build. The golden pheasant hen will hardly pay any attention to a black or light-coloured bantam cock. What is needed is a colourful cock bird, a cock with a touch of blue and white, some red about him, and perhaps a light head. This sort of bird is hard to find.

Running an assortment of bantams and a black cock in the same pen as the pair of golden pheasants had nothing of a scientific approach about it. In fact, it could only lead to the confusion which resulted when I began to think that, casually and without serious intent, I had a cross. It was the finer, pointed shape of some of the bantam eggs that led me down this by-way, and by-way it proved. I gathered the eggs that looked like pheasant-bantam crosses and set them under a bantam hen that had become broody. The chicks hatched in due course. Two of them looked so different from the rest that I was convinced that I had a phantam! What I should have done was to pen the golden pheasant with a hen bantam for a period of sixteen days or more and gather the eggs and set them under a hen. The golden pheasant hen should have been parted from her mate long before the breeding season and run with a bantam cock. In doing things this way I might have set bantam hens to hatch what would prove to be infertile clutches, but at least I should have had a chance of a positive result. My two chicks were part of a clutch of six. After two weeks or so only one seemed to be developing into a phantam. In due course of time the chicks fledged. The 'phantam' had white on the primaries, a bright blue wing and a shade of yellow or pale gold on the head and neck. I watched it day by day. It was a cock bird. Its plumage continued to have an uncanny resemblance to that of the cock golden pheasant. I had never seen a more handsome cockerel. Everyone who saw it remarked on its balanced blue and white marking and its yellow about the head and neck. At six months it crowed the shrill crow of a bantam cock and was larger than its father—the black Rosecomb cockerel. I could delude myself no longer. In the words of Runyon, what I had was a bantam. It looked a bit like a golden pheasant cock, but it looked much more like a bantam cock.

The next step is to provide the pens in which courtship between golden pheasant and suitably coloured bantam hen may take place, and to give the golden pheasant hen an opportunity of mating with a bantam cock. The 'phantam' of the previous season has all the grand points of the golden pheasant cock except crest feathers, long tail and scarlet flanks. I don't think this should prove impossible of attainment. I am fairly sure that the cross can be achieved but it remains to be seen. From there, if all goes well, I must set up pens to check the fertility of the cross, which is a similar experiment and one requiring as much care and patience.

Where do I go from there? I don't know. The business thus far has led me from hawks and quail to sheep and ducks, hens and bantams although the phantam as yet eludes me. In the process of learning about it, and the other creatures I have kept, I have stocked my mind with a great deal of information no one else would carry or even be bothered to research. I freely admit this. The inconsequential fact is discarded by man until, looking for something, he unearths it again and puts it to use, hoping that the ragbag may contain more treasure. I can claim to have made my contribution to the ragbag of knowledge! I know how to make a partridge whistle. I can call owls and pigeons. I know the difference between the alarm conversation of mallards and the reassuring quack that makes a flight turn and swing in to land. I have caught sizeable trout by studying what it is they go for on the surface of a rippled lake—a dimpling and blurred impression on the skin of the water that has nothing to do with the shape of the fly as we see it from above, or its colour. I have studied the behaviour of sheep and the way to handle birds by self-discipline that would please a teacher of yoga, for peace comes from within and radiates its message. So next year, the phantam, and the year after that phantam bred with phantam, if that is possible. Beyond that there may be a world of crossbred ducks, bigger hens, larger eggs, cures for arthritis with bee-stings, cures with honey, for honey was once used to heal wounds and seal them off from bacteria.

I look forward to living and studying life, although I am not sure that all of my fellow men are as intrigued with either as I am. Some are more concerned with death and destruction and I am sorry for them. It seems to me most important to preserve life in all its forms because one form is so well-integrated with another. More than superstition makes me think that it is wrong to break the chain, or try to alter the balance, even though it may be held that we are within it and can only achieve as much damage as predators can inflict on the other species with which they share existence.